D0445125

BRING
YOURSELF

BRING YOURSELF

HOW TO HARNESS THE POWER OF CONNECTION TO NEGOTIATE FEARLESSLY

Mori Taheripour

Avery / an imprint of Penguin Random House / New York

AVERY

An imprint of Penguin Random House LLC
Penguinrandomhouse.com

Copyright © 2020 by Morvarid Taheripour
Penguin supports copyright. Copyright fuels creativity, encourages
diverse voices, promotes free speech, and creates a vibrant culture.
Thank you for buying an authorized edition of this book and for
complying with copyright laws by not reproducing, scanning, or
distributing any part of it in any form without permission. You are
supporting writers and allowing Penguin to continue to publish books
for every reader.

Most Avery books are available at special quantity discounts for
bulk purchase for sales promotions, premiums, fund-raising,
and educational needs. Special books or book excerpts also can be
created to fit specific needs. For details, write SpecialMarkets@
penguinrandomhouse.com.

Library of Congress Cataloging-in-Publication Data

Names: Taheripour, Mori, author.
Title: Bring yourself: how to harness the power of connection to
negotiate fearlessly / Mori Taheripour.
Description: New York: Avery, an imprint of Penguin Random House,
2020. | Includes bibliographical references and index.
Identifiers: LCCN 2019055433 | ISBN 9780525540304 (hardcover) |
ISBN 9780525540311 (ebook)
Subjects: LCSH: Negotiation—Study and teaching.
Classification: LCC BF637.N4 T34 2020 | DDC 302.3—dc23
LC record available at https://lccn.loc.gov/2019055433

Printed in the United States of America
10 9 8 7 6 5 4 3 2 1

Book design by Lorie Pagnozzi

To those who believed in me more than I believed in myself,
you inspired me to set out on this journey and find my truth.

For that I will always be grateful.

contents

Contents

Chapter 10

author's note

interviewed scores of my current and former students as I wrote this book and am greatly appreciative of their willingness to share their stories with me. In some cases, they asked for their names to be changed and I have done so. My classroom can be an intense setting, and trust and safety are critical to me. I have thus changed the names and details of students whose relationship with negotiation I watched play out in person but whom I did not interview for this book. Finally, the exercises I use in my classroom are a key component to my teaching and I would like them to remain so. As a result, I changed the circumstances and details of the exercises you will read about in this book, while remaining true to their essential principles.

introduction

I n a recent class at Wharton, where I teach negotiation, I paired students up and, as usual, gave them a negotiation exercise wherein they each had a role to play. I sent them off to reach a deal in thirty minutes. One participant plays a contractor who is hired to remodel a client's bathroom. The other student plays the client, who's dissatisfied with the contractor because of several missed appointments. When the contractor finally shows up, he uses the wrong kind of tile. The client actually *prefers* the wrong tile. Nevertheless, she wants a 50 percent discount for the work while the contractor expects to be paid in full.

I was surprised to see that one team—Brett and Angela—returned to class after ten minutes without a deal. It's not unusual for students to reach a stalemate, but they usually spend all thirty minutes trying to find a compromise.

By this point in the semester, students had developed reputations. Brett, who played the contractor, was a highly competitive, win-at-all-costs type of negotiator. He was headed to a banking job in Manhattan after graduation, and the guy oozed confidence. Angela, who played the client, was far less tough and had always been more collaborative in class. She was always friendly, but fairly quiet. This was the first time in class when she didn't get to a deal, so I was a bit surprised.

It turned out neither one thought they could find a solution without the other person losing. They believed that the deal had no positive bargaining zone—a term used to describe the opportunity to identify shared interests, allowing negotiators to find common ground and compromise. Brett and Angela concluded that there was no positive bargaining zone early and decided not to waste any more time going back and forth. They agreed to resort to legal action, which is the last option in this particular case.

Brett and Angela were surprised when their classmates trickled in near the end of the time limit, reporting favorable results of their deals. It became clear that this exercise had many possible unique outcomes that made sense for both the contractor and the client. What happened? What had they missed?

Brett was upset because the outcome reaffirmed his reputation as a difficult person. Angela was upset because she'd let her fear and anxiety get the best of her. She planned to go into the male-dominated field of commercial real estate and considered the exercise practice for how not to back down to someone like Brett. At the outset of the exercise when she was first paired with Brett, she told herself, "Nice guys finish last, and tough negotiators win."

So what do you get when you put a fiercely competitive and uncompromising negotiator together with one who is "acting" like an equally competitive and uncompromising negotiator? Deadlock. A lose-lose outcome.

This isn't always the case between two *genuinely* competitive negotiators. Sure, sometimes it ends up in deadlock, but that's true in any negotiation. But when you're just *pretending* to be competitive, you're not going to get your best deal. You must bring the best version of yourself to get the best deal. The fact that Angela was pretending to be someone who she wasn't—tough as nails—instead of using her authentic strength changed the dynamic of the conversation.

I see this pitfall all the time. People like Angela, who are more accommodating in their negotiation style, often try to change. They try to take on a more aggressive persona because they believe competitive negotiators are often the "winners" and the nice guys always lose. They think they have to be uber aggressive, like Kevin O'Leary on *Shark Tank* or sports agent Drew Rosenhaus. They blame their disappointment in negotiation results on the fact that they aren't tough enough. It's a reasonable position, born from eons of social conditioning that says if you encounter a bully on a playground, act tougher than you are. But when you do, you're so busy trying to keep track of your alternate personality that you're less comfortable maneuvering and pivoting as the negotiation demands. Too much pretense doesn't allow for clarity of thought or allow you to be truly present. There are ways to deal with negotiators who bully, and the most powerful among them is understanding your leverage. Negotiating well does not involve pretending to be like them.

The truth is that anyone can be a good negotiator, no matter what their bargaining style or personality. If you blame your negotiation style for the fact that you're not achieving your desired outcomes, and take on a different persona, there's a strong chance that it will backfire on you. When tensions are high, you tend to revert to what's most comfortable and recognizable—you become *more* of yourself, not less. Maybe you bluster, like Angela, but the act doesn't land because ultimately you are who you are. Outwardly, you've now shown what looks like a split personality. It's the gotcha moment for the other side.

I've taught negotiation to nearly five thousand students over the past fifteen years. I teach both undergraduates and graduate students at Wharton, and I teach entrepreneurs in the Goldman Sachs 10,000 Small Businesses program—which is similar to an executive MBA program for small business owners. I've taught in New Orleans, Detroit, New York, and Providence, to name just a few of the cities I visit regularly. I've taught women living in Cairo, banking executives, Chinese real estate investors, nurses, NFL players, and sports agents. And most of them look confused when I talk about the importance of first really knowing yourself and bringing that person to the bargaining table, which I emphasized when we debriefed Brett and Angela's negotiation in class. *What does self-awareness have to do with negotiation?* they wonder, often out loud. *I thought this was a negotiations class, not therapy.*

I assure them that it is, just as I assure you that this is a negotiations book. But it looks a little different than what you might expect. There are four principles in particular that I raise in class and that I will come back to again and again in these pages:

1. Negotiation is first and foremost about human connection

A negotiation, technically defined, is "a discussion aimed at reaching an agreement." Implicit in that definition is a whole slew of "soft" skills: How do you communicate in the discussion? How do you go about aiming for that agreement? Sure, some negotiations involve a whole lot of complicated calculations, but you can be the greatest numbers genius in the world and still blow a negotiation if you're not tuned in to your personal strengths and blind spots, if you don't have the capability to really understand your counterpart's point of view, or if you can't form a positive connection in the course of your communication. IQ counts for little without EQ, or emotional intelligence.

2. Negotiation requires knowing your worth

I spend a great deal of time in class talking about the role of self-worth in negotiation and cannot overstate its relevance. Someone in class once asked, "What's the opposite of someone who lacks self-confidence?" Another student yelled out, "Narcissist," which I found very telling. The answer couldn't be simply "Someone who has confidence"? Shouldn't having self-confidence be a norm rather than a put-down?

When we don't believe in our worth, we don't see our power. Without seeing our power, we can't understand our leverage, and we can't negotiate to our full potential. Sallie Krawcheck, the former head of Citi and Smith Barney, offers one of my favorite examples of this. As (often) the sole woman in the room at the top echelons of Wall Street, she could have downplayed what made her different from her colleagues or seen it as a detriment. Instead, she wrote a book—*Own It: The Power of Women at Work*—about the ways she found power in it. She saw things differently than everyone else, precisely because she is a woman. Her gender gave her leverage.

Self-worth is a key part of the deep reaches of negotiation, but it's also just the beginning. Negotiation is the lens through which people recognize they need to be better, more present listeners. It's the lens through which they recognize that their outsized ego has been hurting—not helping—their bottom line. It's the lens through which they grapple with the scars of their past, helping them see why they are so quick to make assumptions that get in their way. It's the way they explore their ethics and values. Negotiation is the way through which people strengthen their capacity for empathy, a huge asset in any difficult conversation. As my students see their lives through this lens, they come to a greater sense of self-understanding. Their relationships improve, and they find greater success in their professional and even personal lives. I've had spouses of my students approach me to say the class saved their marriage.

It's not uncommon for someone—or several people—to become emotional in my negotiations class, and maybe even to cry. Not because of me, I should note. I'm not a scary teacher who thrives on cutting people down. But neither am I the embodiment of a big warm hug. I care deeply about my classes and push my students hard to bring their full selves. Without exception, the intensity of the experience surprises people. But that's just one of the many misconceptions people have about negotiation, that it's somehow devoid of feeling, that it's impersonal. I've learned that the opposite is true. I've taught people of all ages, genders, and levels of experience, and I've learned that negotiation is a loaded topic no matter the demographic. Negotiation cuts to the core of our sense of self, what we think we're about, and what worries us. This is why it also has such great potential to teach us.

3. Negotiation is something we do all the time

We negotiate when we're toddlers, throwing a tantrum to get our way, and we negotiate when we consider medical intervention at the end of life. We negotiate with our children, parents, in-laws, employees, neighbors, bosses, health care providers, and everyone in between. We negotiate with ourselves all the time. Ideally, we become better at negotiation as our life goes on and we feel more comfortable engaging in it. Ideally, we come to understand that negotiation plays a role in almost everything we do, and that it's intensely personal.

When you have a conversation with competing parts of yourself, that is negotiation. When your kid doesn't want to go to sleep at bedtime, that is negotiation. When you want your dog to come in, but he wants to stay outside, that is negotiation. When you are on the fence about taking a new job and make a list of pros and cons, that is negotiation—before you've even begun to talk about salary. Negotiation is the platform for us to find our voice. Negotiation is decision making, communication, and critical thinking. It's *life*, and the more comfortable we become engaging in the conversation, the more confident we become in our skills, the more we value ourselves, and the more satisfied we become.

4. Anyone can be a good negotiator

I'm often met with a chorus of students— men and women—who say: "I'm a terrible negotiator." "I'm a pushover." "I'm afraid of hard conversations." "I don't like to negotiate because I don't like conflict." There's a long-standing stereotype of the good negotiator as someone who looks like Brett: confident, aggressive, a bit smooth. That's why Angela—who was empathetic and quiet—thought she was in for it. If I accomplish nothing else in this book, I hope it is to put that misconception to bed once and for all. The truth is that people who are deeply empathetic can be great negotiators. In fact, they are some of the best I've known. People who are introverted can be great negotiators—something I know all too well because I am an introvert myself. People who loathe conflict of any sort can be great negotiators, and in fact come to love negotiation when they realize that so much of it is about problem solving. The flip side of this coin is that not everyone who thinks they're a good negotiator actually is. The Bretts of the world have blind spots, too, which can hamper their ability to get a good deal; perhaps their overconfidence keeps them from adequately preparing, or their reputation closes off opportunities. The key is just in understanding yourself, the strengths you genuinely bring, and then bringing it.

*　　*　　*

Like everyone I've taught, my relationship with negotiation has been a lifelong work in progress.

I moved to the United States as a little girl, in 1978, during the Iranian Revolution. My parents maintained a traditional household, and I was expected to play a dutiful role within it. When there was a disagreement among my parents, my brother, my sister, or me, the rift was not brokered through collaborative problem solving but through impassioned exchanges. Rarely would anyone move from their position, and if the conversations were politically charged or regarding life choices, they were exhausting. We didn't often debate to resolve disagreements. I think we just wanted to express our opinions, even if the result was just another unresolved dispute. Not much fun or efficient, but that was how we communicated and so I learned to pick my battles.

My most memorable encounters with negotiation outside my limited family sphere came when I worked in an HIV education, prevention, and outreach organization in Oakland, California. AIDS/HIV was rampant, and hard-to-reach African American and Latino women, youth, and men who had sex with men were disproportionately affected.

We sought to reach marginalized populations, including prostitutes and their sexual partners, IV drug users, transgender people, and high-risk youth. The effectiveness of our work was attributed to the fact that we met people where they were, on their turf, and provided culturally appropriate, nonjudgmental outreach and education. We understood the population we served. Whether they needed warm meals, clean needles, condoms, financial incentives, or help navigating health care and access to housing, we provided it. We weren't aggressive or critical; we were respectful and compassionate.

Some of my most rewarding yet challenging negotiation experiences came from working in that organization. Talking to prostitutes and substance abusers about the importance of using condoms and clean needles was not your average bargaining scenario. Convincing at-risk youth to get HIV tested and that safe sex was the difference between life and death made for some very interesting conversations. The clients had arrived at that moment from lives lived so differently than mine, but I remember how much I wanted to understand them and their choices, not from a place of condemnation but in a way that I could garner their trust and dignify them by showing my commitment to their well-being. I was just barely twenty-one, and trying to talk strangers into getting a test they really didn't want to get, and to confront an alarming problem they really didn't want to face. In short, it was a crash course in negotiation.

I'll never forget talking to a kid one day—he wasn't much older than eighteen—who wasn't using condoms. As I explained the risk of HIV infection, I could tell he wasn't convinced. "So if I get HIV, how long can I live with it?" he asked. I looked at him quizzically, and he asked again. "If I'm HIV positive, how long until it kills me?"

I remember telling him, as I would anyone who asked the same question, that it's different for everyone and that generally, the time it takes to go from HIV infection to AIDS is around five to ten years without medical treatment. In other words, I answered his question very technically. But the response I got to this information caught me off-guard.

He simply shrugged and said with indifference, "Oh, that's a long time. I can walk out of my house and get shot tomorrow."

I understood then that I could not hope to persuade this kid of anything until I really understood his life. Until I learned enough to walk in his shoes. I could make no assumptions, even very basic ones about risk. It was a lesson I never forgot.

The years of my life in between my grassroots HIV education work and teaching negotiation at Wharton don't look much like those of my professorial colleagues. While I did get an MBA, my work experience focused not on brokering international diplomatic deals but on running my own company, where I learned many business skills on the job, and in advisory roles for companies regarding issues of diversity and inclusion (D&I). If the connection between D&I work and bargaining seems shaky, it actually makes perfect sense: People are different, there's value to be gained in those differences, and in order to uncover and benefit from those differences, you have to be persuasive and negotiate effectively while bringing your full, authentic self.

Then when I began to teach negotiation, I understood there was yet more to it. I looked at my classes as a sort of petri dish. The classes are experiential, where I would send students off to do mock negotiations like the one that opened this chapter and put into practice the theories that I had just taught them. When they returned, I would project everyone's results on a screen so the whole class could view them together. As a student you could instantly see how you'd done compared with other people who had been assigned the same role. But as we went through and examined the outcomes, people would see that a favorable result didn't necessarily mean a win. This process wasn't designed to shame anyone but rather to crack the whole process open. The methodology makes people feel exposed, and that vulnerability, if facilitated effectively, results in unusual and often unexpected frankness.

As we debriefed, I noticed that my students struggled with similar obstacles, and that there was more to the story than the numbers showed. I prodded and analyzed to get deeper into it. Some set their asks too low, and I saw the correlation between what they asked for and how they felt about themselves. Others would "try on" different personas like Angela did, thinking that they needed to be tough in order to do well in a negotiation, and it rarely worked. I noticed how increasingly distracted many of my students were over the years, and how they were missing key information that could be detrimental to their outcome because they couldn't keep their focus on their counterpart. I also knew that coming into the class, many viewed bargaining as a battleground with winners and losers, not as a conversation that could lead to mutual gain.

As I focused more on my students' tendencies, I changed the way I taught my class. I still talked about standard concepts like the importance of using data to set a goal, but I focused more on the story people saw when they looked at that data, and why. The energy in my classroom changed. People began to know one another better, to be vulnerable with one another, and to uncoil some troublesome habits that had been holding them back. Whereas some negotiations professors graded students according to their outcomes in mock negotiations, I thought there was a better way—a way that focused more on the process.

When students say of my class, "Wow, that wasn't at all what I expected," I get it. It's not what I expected, either. And the truth is that I still don't know what to expect—that's why I feel a little uncomfortable when anyone describes me as an "expert." I don't think it's possible to be an expert in negotiation, because I get a richer, more nuanced understanding of it every day. We all do.

You won't see a lot of theory or prescriptive advice in this book. Plenty of books offer that, and do it well. What you will see, in part because it's what my students have asked for, is scenarios—the practical application of the very human machinations going on under the surface of the many negotiations of our lives.

Part I of this book delves into what gets us into trouble as negotiators and includes the patterns I notice most often. Chapter 1 focuses on the stories we tell ourselves about our worth and how those stories color what we ask for, whether it's claiming a day to ourselves or asking for a raise. In Chapter 2, I look at what happens when a need to be liked interferes with our ability to look out for our interests. Chapter 3 covers the impact of painful experiences in the way we negotiate with ourselves and the world around us, while Chapter 4 emphasizes that people too frequently focus on what they want to ask for but not how they should ask for it.

Part II of the book moves the conversation forward, beyond what holds us back and toward what gets us to *yes*—and even further. Effective negotiators aim to get more than they initially planned, and to get that for everyone.

I think of Chapters 5, 6, and 7 as a triad, as they cover the integrated skills of open-mindedness, empathy, and presence. You have to begin every negotiation with curiosity, with exchanging information openly. You can learn more about where your counterpart is coming from when you have shown authentic interest and the capacity to make the conversation about more than just a transaction. You show empathy so that even if their view is wildly different from your own, you can grasp why they've taken it. Presence is critical in the process, as you have to work on effectively being in the moment and reading the cues of your partner. Presence allows your counterpart to believe that you are authentically interested in them and what they have to say.

Open-mindedness, empathy, and presence enable us to do the

problem solving I tackle in Chapter 8, to sort through concessions, and to assume that the pie is big enough for all of us to have a slice.

In Chapter 9, the principles of Chapters 1 through 8 culminate with the idea that when you find your power, you have leverage—which has a much deeper meaning than just who can bring more money or resources to bear.

In the final chapter, Chapter 10, I take all that I've covered and apply it to the minefield of our democracy. Because in a nation—really, a world—of constant conflict, it's more critical than ever that we explore ways to come to the table.

Throughout the book, you'll read stories of my students and the ways they've struggled—as I did—to negotiate with their parents' expectations, but you'll also read about football stars who similarly struggle to communicate their value. You'll read stories of middle-aged parents figuring out child care, and twenty-year-olds trying to figure out their lives. You'll read about negotiation luminaries like Nelson Mandela, and small business owners like Sarah Farzam whom you've never heard of. And through these stories it will become clear to you that we are all struggling with the same things—and it will become clear that our struggles with negotiation begin with us.

part I

what gets in our way

WHAT YOU'RE THINKING
IS WHAT YOU'RE
BECOMING.
—MUHAMMAD ALI

CHAPTER 1

how our stories sell us short

My life's most significant negotiation was with myself.

It started with some numbness in my hands, a nuisance I didn't have time for. It was 2010, and I was in the middle of one of the most stressful periods I'd ever encountered with the company I cofounded. I was not only writing a proposal for a big contract but also deciding if I wanted to try to salvage the struggling company or move on. The numbness in my hands would have to wait. But when the proposal was submitted and the numbness worsened, I knew I had to see a doctor. At the back of my mind was the optic neuritis—swelling of the optic nerve—that I'd had eight years prior. The doctor had said then that it might be a sign of multiple sclerosis (MS), which we then ruled out. Numb hands seemed like another sign. Denial and avoidance were tempting companions, but I knew it was better to know than not, so I got an MRI and was referred to a neurologist.

The neurologist who gave me my diagnosis was very matter-of-fact. All I remember is hearing that I had MS and that I would need steroid injections immediately to address the numbness. Although I seemed like a rock on the outside, the opposite was true within. Over the next week or so, my skin broke out badly and I lost my appetite. My best friend just happened to be visiting me and helped with the initial treatments. I felt weak and dependent—two feelings that I had always fiercely fought. In retrospect, I realize how tormented I was, how afraid of my reality. The vision I had of people living with MS was of them being in wheelchairs and having limited mobility and independence. I had no idea what my diagnosis meant, or what my future looked like, and I was afraid that I would someday become dependent on others for my basic needs. In the absence of knowledge about MS, the story I told myself in this vulnerable moment was of the horror variety. I found information that only validated my fears and rejected all other information. I limited the possibilities. I became my own worst enemy.

But things looked up soon. I searched for the most expert care available and had the good fortune of getting an appointment with one of the best neurologists in D.C. As soon as he shook my hand and welcomed me to his office, it felt as though I had a shawl to wrap myself in. I saw compassion in his eyes, and somehow I felt safe. This doctor proceeded to spend what seemed an eternity with me. I sat beside him as he took me through my MRI on the computer screen. He gave me explanation on top of explanation and quickly chipped away at the dreadful information I had found on the Internet. "I'm in the business of creating possibilities," he explained, "not in limiting them." He told me that he was going to do everything he could to ensure that I would remain healthy and avoid a relapse, but he was also clear that his recommended treatment was intense. "I would prefer to be aggressive," he said, "because I want you to remain as healthy as you are today."

He pointed out a critical piece of data that my doomsday narrative had missed: "If you actually had your first flare-up eight years ago and haven't had one since even though you haven't been on any treatment, that tells us something. The healthy lifestyle that you have led, be it working out or having good eating habits, has helped to keep you healthy and your body strong. That's pretty amazing if you think about it."

And that was all it took. I had the biggest "aha" moment of my life. This doctor helped me see that I needed to change the story, and to tell a truer one. My entire spirit shifted. I felt like my old self for the first time in weeks. I felt strong, determined, focused, and oddly healthy. The difference was so immediate and stark that it was almost like an out-of-body experience.

Just as I explain to my students, I had to look at the information I had before me and grasp how to weigh it. This godsend of a neurologist was right. I had been symptom-free for eight years, and that was pretty amazing. Why did I so quickly discount that piece of data?

From that moment on, I've had a very clear story. Yes, I am living with MS—that part hasn't changed. But I am healthy, and my diagnosis has actually been a gift that has helped me prioritize my health. In the life of an entrepreneur where work/life balance is impossible at times, my health never takes a back seat. Eight years later, I remain symptom-free. I am perhaps healthier and in better shape than I have *ever* been in, and I often forget that I am living with MS. There is nothing that I can't do physically, and the limits that I push myself to sometimes surprise me. In fact, when most of my friends, family, colleagues, and students read this, they will be shocked because they didn't know. I haven't been open about it because I don't want it to define me or to alter the way people see me.

My doctor tells me that, given how long it's been since a relapse, he expects I'll continue to stay this healthy. In many ways, I'm living as my best self. Fearless and determined. Influenced profoundly by hope and possibility and not by fear. The story I told myself on that fateful day in 2010 has never changed.

In my work teaching negotiation, I serve the same role for my students that my neurologist served for me. I often encounter my students when they are vulnerable and unsure. I hear all kinds of stories from them: They are the youngest person in their field and can't compete; they are the only person of color or the only woman; they are "just" a hairdresser or a chef. They haven't questioned these stories and don't expect a negotiations class to be the place where they'll do so. By far, the most common story I hear is one that sells their value short. And like my neurologist, I say, "Why do you believe that? Why can't you see what I see? Let's look at all the facts here. Let's be in the business of creating possibilities."

It was a sunny, beautiful afternoon in Baltimore, and a graduation rehearsal was in full swing for the Goldman Sachs 10,000 Small Businesses program's first two cohorts. The program is an investment by Goldman Sachs to help entrepreneurs grow their companies and add jobs. In addition to the classroom component that I teach in, the students receive access to capital and opportunities for some pretty invaluable networking. I'd be a huge fan of the program even if I didn't teach for it. On the day I was visiting Baltimore, the students laughed easily, excited to share the graduation celebration with their families the following day. Since they worked full-time jobs (and then some) while attending, getting through had not been an easy feat. They had every reason to be in party mode.

Outside the rehearsal, I ran into one of my students, Dana Sicko. She was energetic and smiley, and I always thought of her as upbeat. She owned a catering company and a juice company and, like the flavors of her drinks, her energy defied the size of the package it came in. That afternoon, though, she looked different. She looked small, and maybe even a little anxious—more like a little girl than the impressive woman I knew her to be. Her demeanor was such a striking contrast to the revelry at the rehearsal, and to how I was used to seeing Dana, so I went over to see what was up.

We chatted amiably for a minute or two, and she seemed distracted, like she was trying to put on a happy face for me. I started talking about something I knew we were both passionate about: juice cleanses.

"You know I'm a big juicer, right?" I said. I've long been a health nut and consider myself a connoisseur of fresh-pressed juice.

"Oh," she said, "I'm not sure I did know that. What are some of your favorites?"

I listed one or two before saying, "But one of my favorites is Gundalow."

She nodded politely, and it was like she didn't even hear what I'd said. After maybe a minute she said, surprised, "Wait—that's *my* company."

"I know," I responded. I thought, *Is this woman crazy? Does she really not get what an amazing product she has?*

As I found out later, Dana was worried about Gundalow. The company was facing a series of challenges, and she wasn't sure it would stay in business. Instead of looking forward to her graduation from the program, she felt like a fraud. When I encountered her that day, she was imagining what it would feel like to walk across the graduation stage and pretend she was a success, when she was sure she was not.

This narrative—more than the actual numbers for the business—was a very real threat to Gundalow. Dana was in the midst of putting together a forecast for her investors and needed to determine where to anchor their sales. She could focus on the not-so-great year behind the company, or the year before *that*, when it'd soared, and she could also take into account the logistical obstacles that had slowed the company's progress but that now lay behind it. Changing her mind-set did not mean putting on a false persona, pretending to be confident when she wasn't. It meant actually *being* confident, challenging some of the assumptions she was making, and looking at *all* the information in front of her, not just pieces that looked bad. The day we chatted was a low one for Dana. But before putting together her investment forecast, Dana recalibrated and drew on what she'd learned in class. She considered a broader set of facts, not just what hurt her, and presented an optimistic story that was completely justified.

What's your story?

We can be our own worst enemy in negotiation because of the stories we tell ourselves. More often than not, those stories sell us short.

I am not preaching from a perch of perfection when I say this. I have told myself plenty of unhelpful stories about my value. For years, I was in business with a partner who was older and more experienced than I was. He was my mentor early in my career, before we went into business together, and as a result I was overly deferential. When business was good, the differences in our decision making weren't so obvious, but when we hit major road bumps and financial challenges, the disparity in our approach was clear. In those tough times, I felt the burden of our debt and the guilt associated with the impending layoffs of our employees. I was always worried and felt the weight of our obligations in a very personal way, while his years of experience made him more cavalier. It was difficult to make joint decisions about how to honor our financial commitments when we had totally different feelings about accountability.

I deferred to him instead of standing my ground because of the story I told myself: *I still have a lot to learn. I lack self-confidence. I am young and naïve.* I could have told myself a different story: *Yes, he's more experienced in some areas. But I have great instincts and intellect, and I was responsible for bringing in our seed funding to launch the business.* I certainly wouldn't have done everything right—in hindsight, for instance, he was absolutely correct about not taking on the financial burden of our employees—but when I look back on that time in my life as a young entrepreneur, I regret that I didn't rest in my power more fully.

In the uncertain faces of students like Dana, I see myself and I want to help them avoid the self-doubt that plagued me at many points of my life. If I can't offer a magic path over it, I at least want to help them recognize their self-doubt, to examine it, to know that it's there so they can figure out what to do about it. Because if it's the story they're telling themselves, they're also projecting their insecurities. That's why the most common refrain I offer my students is, "You can't be the person who diminishes your value—others will too often do that for you."

A woman in one of my classes, Kim, acknowledged that she felt a distinct lack of confidence, and she went on to put herself down for failing to "hold her ground" in a negotiation. And yet even before meeting Kim, I could see that she had a magnetic quality to her. In the prep I'd done for the class, Kim's photo stood out to me. She had a commanding smile, in which I saw confidence and poise. When we later discussed her internal uncertainty, I said, "Let me tell you how I saw you before we even met." Simply hearing how she was perceived in that photo—as strong and commanding—made her break into tears. It was how she wanted to *feel*. She understood that the work she needed to do in class had much less to do with calculations and posturing, and more to do with believing her value.

This was by no means the only time I had an interaction like this—it happens all the time, where I will observe someone in a complimentary way and it touches a nerve that is so raw, they become emotional. In another recent encounter, I asked a student why her opening ask was so low. "Maybe I didn't understand the case," she said. She paused, then added, "Maybe I didn't think I deserved more."

I knew she was an accomplished businesswoman, so I said, "Don't you have twenty years of experience running a company? Who can do this better than you? Why do you think you don't deserve it?"

"I wish I could tell you," she said. "I just don't think I do."

Lest you assume this is a women's issue, note that I see it all the time with men, including the most stereotypically masculine of men: NFL players. I have worked with them when they were preparing for their transition out of the NFL, looking ahead to a future that is honestly very scary and uncertain. When they leave the sport, they have to be their own cheering section, likely for the first time in their lives, since so many of them were revered high school and college athletes. That is a lonely, frightening place to stand, and that loneliness makes it much easier to be their own worst enemy. A moment of self-doubt creeps in, and the enemy within exploits it.

"I don't have any experience besides football," they say. "That's what I'm good at. That's all I know."

Those of us who work with athletes see it differently. Being on a team is phenomenal work experience. Athletes don't think they have skills that translate to the wider world? What about discipline? Collaboration? Grit? Resilience? The ability to memorize complicated playbooks? To watch and break down hours of film? Work ethic? Everything they've done to prepare for the "one thing" they say they're good at has so much relevance, whether they want to go work for a company or start their own. They've just selectively edited it out of the story they've told themselves.

The stories we tell ourselves shape and define us and impact how we negotiate with the world around us. When you grasp this concept, you begin to see it everywhere—in classes you take, in people you work with, and in television shows you watch. One of my favorite shows focusing on this theme is *The Marvelous Mrs. Maisel*, wherein the heroine, Midge Maisel, appears to have her story written for her. She is an upper-middle-class housewife living in New York in the late 1950s, filling the supportive role that a wife of the era was expected to (including not putting on face cream or rolling her hair until after her husband falls asleep, so as not to ruin the picture of perfection). When her husband announces he's had an affair and is leaving her, Midge's story still seems predetermined: She should keep up appearances until he comes to his senses, and then she should take him back. But she wants more. She recognizes she *is* more. She is funny and bright and she wants to be a stand-up comic. She doesn't allow herself to be defined by the obstacles in her life or the traditions of her era. Her story evolved from one of "I am a devoted mom and homemaker" to "I am a devoted mom and homemaker and comic—and nothing is going to stop me," which then becomes, "Nothing's going to stop me."

Television shows make it all look so easy, character development compacted into an eight-hour season. But make no mistake—it is not. Telling yourself the right story is actually messy and complicated and, while necessary, also incredibly hard. It is self-esteem, self-awareness, and battling of imposter syndrome all rolled into one. The story of your value is also not a "Kumbaya," "love yourself" lesson meant for yoga retreats in Sedona and nowhere else. It's a very practical one, and it has everything to do with how we negotiate. If self-doubt drives our negotiations, we start determining the outcomes of a negotiation before we even begin. And the more confident you are about what your story is, the less vulnerable you are to those who would question it. The stories we tell ourselves can make the difference between a great outcome and a bad one, between going onstage and going home.

The bottom line: If you expect less, you ask for less, and you receive less

There is a category of negotiator I think of as the "good enough" people. They don't set aspirational goals, they play it safe, and when they (inevitably) get offered less, they accept the deal. What makes "good enough" people tricky to spot is that they never explain their reasoning that way. They never would say, "I'm happy with good enough." Instead, they rationalize their approach by arguing that they didn't have favorable data to support a larger ask, or that they did only what was ethical. The rationalizations are many and varied, but underlying them is a story that mediocre is fine and that good is great.

Sam, a Wharton undergraduate, was one such student. He didn't like to make waves and although he usually came away from mock negotiations having made a deal, he never made a very good one. In one class exercise, he played the seller of a condo. The condo had a beautiful and hard-to-come-by view of the water, which was its great selling point. But the building was also in need of new siding, which meant that all unit owners would be slapped with a hefty "special assessment" fee and be subject to months of annoying construction.

Sam's bottom line was $300,000. Like all of the exercises I use, students had enough information to safely make a value assumption. Sam determined that if he sold the condo for less, he'd lose too much money. The price he offered to the buyer was $325,000, and he spent a long time explaining how special assessments hit every condo building on occasion, and that this one wasn't such a big deal in the long term. The buyer, Jane, wouldn't pay more than $290,000, and Sam came out on the losing end. "Why did you even bother to make this deal? Why not just wait for another potential buyer?" I asked when we went over it in class. "You could have just walked away."

Sam looked decidedly upset after class, and so I asked if he wanted to talk about it. "Selling myself short is for sure a recurring issue for me, isn't it?" he asked. I had to agree. Whenever Sam had something to sell, it went poorly. His sticking point was always the same: He could not embrace his own value in a negotiation, and so whatever he got was "good enough."

As students like Sam prepare for the case, they don't focus primarily on how to use the information they have to set more aspirational goals (the condo has a killer view!). Instead, they spend just as much time finding the holes in their argument (the assessment! the construction!) and wondering what their counterpart will think. "Given the issues with the condo, how can I come up with a high offer?" "Am I being too greedy?" "How do I truly know the appropriate value of the condo?" Self-doubt creeps in, and the outcome is a safe ask or opening offer.

When we debriefed the exercise, Sam, predictably, said there simply wasn't enough data to support a higher ask. He didn't think he could justify it. "All right," I said. "Let's test that." Together we ran through the data he'd been given ahead of time, data that showed condos in that same neighborhood selling for $350,000 or $400,000. "Yes," he said, "but they were all bigger." This was a powerful "diagnosis" moment. This is where Sam kept getting stuck, and it happens with students who question their value all the time. They latch on to the one or two pieces of data that would weaken their position, instead of spending the time identifying and finding ways to justify a stronger ask—which they have an equal amount of information to support.

Sam's opening offer came from a place of fear of the judgment he might invite from the other side, and fear of being discredited. Those who have a healthier sense of worth and belief in their assumptions do just the opposite. They start their preparation by identifying their value and the strength of their asset(s), then devising the argument that will persuade their counterpart. They do consider the counterarguments. But they don't consider them *first*. That order of thought makes a huge difference. They don't start from a point of fear and weakness but rather confidence and leverage.

Sam watched as other students debriefed and saw that sellers who got $320,000 or more for the condo had legitimate arguments for why the property was worth so much, such as its fantastic view or its hardwood floors. "Oh," he said, starting to put it all together. "I guess I just didn't consider those aspects."

Sam's recognition started in class, but it couldn't end there. The condo sale was just an exercise and had nothing to do with his daily life. But the lesson had to do with his habits outside class. This is true of almost every exercise that we run, which makes them such powerful learning opportunities. Undervaluing yourself, doubting your self-worth based on the perceived stereotypes or perceptions of others, is destructive. The ideal opening offer is one that is built on the premise of a really strong, data-driven goal that you can stand behind logically with aspirational and persuasive storytelling. Starting from this frame of mind makes it easier to communicate to your counterpart and easier for you to hold ground.

A tale of two babysitters and the pitfalls of working for free

We begin programming our stories very early in life, and then we tend to stick to them. Look no further than this story of two babysitters:

Jenna asked her thirteen-year-old neighbor Madeline if she might babysit Jenna's two daughters one afternoon. Madeline said yes. Jenna asked Madeline how much she charged per hour, as she wanted to be sure to have the correct amount of cash on hand. "I don't know," Madeline said awkwardly. "Just pay me whatever you think is right."

"What do the other parents you babysit for pay you?" Jenna pressed.

Madeline shrugged. She was red by now. "Just whatever they think, I guess." She studied her shoes closely, signaling: *I do not want to talk about this. Do not make me talk about money. Just let this conversation be over!*

Madeline was letting other people define her value. She probably thought, *I'm just thirteen, what do I know?* Well, she knows enough to be left in charge of Jenna's children, so that's saying something.

Contrast this with another babysitter of Jenna's, Dawn. In this case, Dawn watched the girls every afternoon for a week, and described her fee at the outset of the week, explaining that it was market rate for thirteen-year-olds, then adding that she had taken a babysitting class at a nearby hospital. When Jenna paid her at the end of the week, Dawn said, "Oh, you're short by five dollars." Dawn's mother, who was there to pick her up, was mortified and quick to apologize for her daughter.

Jenna told Dawn's mother not to say anything, fixed the discrepancy, and tipped Dawn generously—she was that happy to see a young woman be assertive.

I don't want to be too hard on thirteen-year-olds, who have it tough enough as it is. But these thirteen-year-olds become twenty-two-year-olds who sign up for internships, then get entry-level jobs, and later become executives working their way up the corporate ladder. Understanding their value in the economy is crucial, and adjusting it as they grow is, too. Note that I'm not talking about entitlement. A twenty-two-year-old with no work experience is no more entitled to a managerial job than Dawn would be entitled to a $20/hour babysitting gig. You've got to be able to back it up, but you must start from a place of knowing your value. Note that Dawn had information that supported her ask. She knew the market rate for sitters, and she knew what she was bringing to the table. At thirteen, she understood her value.

One of my students, Sarah Farzam, started her company, Bilingual Birdies—a program that teaches languages to children through song—when she was just twenty-four. "In the beginning," Sarah said, "parents would drop their kids off and they'd say, 'Who's running this joint?' And I'd say, 'Uh, me.'"

Negotiation of any sort, Sarah said, filled her with dread. "I was afraid of *no* because I didn't have much awareness of what my worth was." Undoubtedly, those she negotiated with could sense it. So she went to SCORE, which offers free small business advice, and she was paired with an accomplished executive mentor, an older man who ran a software company.

"I would go in to meet him wearing my little Forever 21 clothes," Sarah said. "And I'd say, 'How do you talk about money in a meeting?' And he'd say, 'What do you mean? You just talk about it.' And I said, 'I can't do that.'" As he casually tossed a miniature ball in his office basketball hoop, he explained, "All you do is tell someone, 'My fee for this is $1,000,' or whatever."

Sarah thought, *This man comes from a different planet from me. He has no fear. There has been some disconnect along the way. He is so confident and I am so sure I can't do this.*

No offense to this SCORE guy (well, that's not totally true), but he was oblivious. He didn't grasp Sarah's issue, which was that she was telling herself a story wherein she was an inexperienced child asking for money from grown-ups. Without getting to the root of Sarah's story and helping her see a different one—that she was immensely capable, energetic, spoke four languages, and was a gifted teacher—he couldn't help her negotiate. She couldn't just state her fee; she had to believe she was *worth* that fee.

Sarah's struggle is common. Just consider how many people give away their work product for free. I constantly hear justifications like, "Oh, I don't want their money—it didn't take me much time to help them," or "I was happy to do it," or "They had a worthy cause, so I was okay helping them." All of these things may indeed be true, and I'm not trying to make you into *Wall Street*'s Gordon Gekko, who famously bragged, "Greed, for lack of a better word, is good." By all means, be a charitable person! Yet I'm a big believer in always getting paid *something*, even if it's small, or at the very least being intentional about donations of your work (e.g., setting a cap of two pro bono projects a year). Your time is valuable because *you* are valuable, and that's an important message to send to the world and to yourself. Your time is not free—there is a cost.

I typically hire my former students to work as teacher's assistants for me. Almost without fail, when I ask them their rate, they say, "Oh, I don't need to get paid. It's just a great opportunity to work with you."

I always respond, "If you don't want any money, then I'm not going to hire you, because you're going to go through life thinking that people don't value your time and your effort. And I want you to understand that I value your time and your effort, and my simply *saying* that isn't enough." I understand their inclination, though. If I were in my twenties again and my professor offered me a job, I wouldn't immediately say, "How much are you paying me?" The psyche of saying "I don't need to get paid" makes perfect sense. But these proclamations become habit-forming, and when they become subconscious, they also become dangerous.

The process of undercutting your value is very subtle—it starts as a tiny snowball that then collects more and more momentum until it's become a dangerous avalanche. Here's how it might go: Perhaps you're concerned about your ability to attract clients, so when you offer a proposal for your work, the proposal includes a lot of your valuable knowledge. You feel you need to overperform and blow their socks off—you don't trust that you're compelling enough for them to take a risk by hiring you. The problem is, you're so concerned about proving yourself that you've just given all of your value away. Why would they pay you when you will offer so much for free?

When they won't pay for your knowledge, it then undermines your value even more. Perhaps you drop your price down for the next potential client. Your course has been set, and it's difficult to change. Others will see that you don't think much of your value, and they'll take advantage, because people will take what you give them.

My philosophy is, let there be some exchange of value, even if it's not monetary. For instance, if I asked a former student to do a small job for me, I would hope that he would at least say, "I don't want money, but will you write me a letter of recommendation for law school, which I know will take you time?" There has to be some level of back-and-forth, of give-and-take, so that you don't subconsciously decrease what your worth actually is.

There are many smart reasons to work without compensation of a financial nature. You may want to make yourself relevant to an organization. You may be able to put the company's name on your client list, which increases your brand's legitimacy. The work itself may bring you fulfillment. And if you walk away without a paycheck, you've still come out ahead.

These reasons did not exist for Jeremy. Jeremy sold municipal bonds, and part of his great strength as a salesman was his ability to develop relationships with clients. He hit it off personally with a large potential client, who started to call and ask him for help. Jeremy gave it willingly and suggested they get a contract going. The potential client said, "Yes, definitely, we're working on that on our end." On and on it went, with Jeremy continuing to do unpaid work, and the potential client continuing to delay the contract process. This is incredibly common, and I'm guessing you can see where this story is headed: When they finally got around to the contract stage, the client balked at Jeremy's fees. The relationship fell apart, with Jeremy feeling used and the client feeling angered that he'd charge so much—especially for work the client clearly hadn't valued all along.

Jeremy was right to put time and energy into developing the relationship. His mistake was in letting the unpaid work go on for so long, and without clearly indicating the value he was bringing to the client. He needed to have educated the consumer, so to speak. Jeremy's potential client never understood all that he'd given.

Jeremy's greatest task once things fell apart was to understand that he'd learned a valuable lesson that might save him money in the long term. He had to fight against having a chip on his shoulder, assuming that everyone going forward would try to take advantage of him. That would be a scar that harmed his judgment, which I'll get into more in Chapter 3.

The bottom line is that you have to be very thoughtful in making decisions about what you're giving up, the effort you're putting in, and what you may be getting in return. It's not opportunistic so much as it's strategic. It's also about honoring yourself and the value you're expending. A transaction is never just about a financial gain but rather about the reciprocity of respect for one another's value. Checking in with yourself regularly to ensure that you're finding fulfillment and that you're valued—whether it's in the form of compensation, a relationship, or a learning opportunity—is critical. If you don't feel valued, and yet you continue to give, you may begin to doubt your worth, leading to habits that further the negative cycle. Alternatively, you may become resentful, which is equally detrimental.

It's particularly easy to fall into bad habits in a down economy, where you give one or two people a deal and then the new price becomes their expectation, or worse, *yours*. Don't punish yourself if you've done this—a lot of entrepreneurs and small business owners are particularly vulnerable to this thinking as they struggle through rough financial patches or attempt to attract clients. It's called survival!

Nevertheless, you have to ensure that your clients don't continue to expect the deep discounts. I was always impressed by the way my gym's spa in D.C. walked this line. It ran a special during the long period of the economic downswing, wherein it advertised an eighty-minute massage for the price of sixty minutes, billed as "the monthly special." This went on for a long time, given the longevity of the weakened economy. When the economy recovered, the special stopped, too. Note that the price of an eighty-minute massage had never changed—it had been offered for less as a "temporary" deal because it was labeled as such. Customers weren't mad when the deal went away, because the gym had always communicated that it was a monthly special. The sale went away and so did our expectations.

How gender directs our stories

Self-doubt is not confined to any one gender, but gender nevertheless plays a strong role in the stories I hear. At the beginning of class, many women announce that they're not good negotiators or that they have "negotiation-induced anxiety." Or they keep this thought to themselves, but when I share the outcome of the first negotiation, they're upset if it's not tilted in their favor. It has reinforced for them what they were already afraid of—that they're not cut out for negotiating. They are so extremely hard on themselves. When I point out ways they could have gotten a better deal, they nod and say, "I know. I should have done better."

In contrast, when I point out to the men in the classroom that they could have done better, many say, "Yeah, but in my defense, look how well I did at this other part." They'll say this even if they didn't get a good outcome. In a recent class I said to one such student, "Chris, you've got some room for improvement." He had gotten an okay deal in our mock negotiation, but he hadn't taken some variables into account, and he hadn't asked enough questions of the person he was negotiating with, questions that would have led to even more potential solutions and a better deal for Chris.

Chris got pretty defensive, so I said, "Don't take what I said personally. Everyone has room for improvement and I'm just trying to help you get better—that's what this is all about." And, because I rarely hold anything back in my classes, I observed how many of the guys in class who hadn't done that well reacted similarly, adding, "The men in this room are confident and focus on what they did do well instead of holding on to their missteps, even if their outcomes aren't great."

"Hey!" said another guy. "I take offense to that." Here we go again!

"Don't," I said. "I mean it as a compliment." Then I addressed the women. "Ladies, if we only had a quarter of the confidence the men in this room have, just think of what that would do for our self-esteem. I'm not looking for behavior change in the men. But I am looking for transformations in the women. You all are acting like this one result is framing you as a negotiator for the rest of your lives. You look for weaknesses instead of celebrating your strengths."

Research backs up my anecdotal observations. In a fascinating study, researchers formed MBA students into groups that worked closely together throughout a year. At the end of each quarter, each student assessed their own performance and received a peer review. Both men and women rated themselves more highly than their peers did. However, on seeing the feedback, the women brought their self-evaluation scores down the following quarters. Men did, too, but not nearly as much. "We found that women more quickly aligned their self-awareness with peer feedback, whereas men continued to rationalize and inflate their self-image over time," the lead researcher, Margarita Mayo, wrote in the *Harvard Business Review*. "That is, in our survey, women were a lot more sensitive to peer feedback than men. After six months, women perfectly aligned their views of leadership with their peers' assessment. In contrast, men continued to inflate their leadership qualities."

There are several ways to look at this. At one level, it certainly suggests that women are more self-aware, which is a great quality for a negotiator. On the other hand, as Mayo points out, "when assimilation of negative feedback involves doubts about one's competences and lowers confidence, it can discourage women to take on new challenges." The authors of *The Confidence Code*, Katty Kay and Claire Shipman, back this up: "The data is pretty grim," they write. "Compared with men, we don't consider ourselves ready for promotions, we predict we'll do worse on tests, we flat out tell researchers in big numbers that we just don't feel confident at our jobs." If women don't feel as confident in their jobs, what does that say about the confidence they have placing a high value in a negotiation?

When she was growing up, my Goldman Sachs 10,000 Small Businesses student Dana Sicko would apologize all the time. She would start conversations or emails with, "I'm sorry to bother you, but . . ." or "Sorry to be a pest, but . . ." or "I'm sorry if you've already thought about this, but . . ." She diminished her own credibility by apologizing before she started talking. So many women do this, and I've been guilty of it myself plenty of times. According to research in *Psychological Science*, women apologize more because they see more incidents as worthy of apology than men do. It's like we always think we're inconveniencing people.

As Dana's confidence grew over the years, she was able to start asking for what she really wanted without prefacing anything with an apology. "It doesn't make me a bad person to speak out for myself," she said. "I can say, 'I'm not ready to budge on this part of a deal, but we can come together on this.' I apologize a lot less now."

I know how impactful these gendered stories can be because I've seen the changes again and again when women question their narratives or completely gut them. Perhaps the most memorable experience I ever had involving gender issues was when I taught at the American University in Cairo (AUC) for the Goldman Sachs 10,000 Women program, a global program where female entrepreneurs are provided with business education, mentoring and networking, and access to capital. The women in the program came to AUC from across the Arab region for this once-in-a-lifetime chance to take their businesses to the next level. The program provided them a much-needed community of like-minded individuals who could share their experiences and challenges, a place where they could find validation for their entrepreneurial goals and vision.

The lofty academic surroundings of AUC were certainly intimidating at first. For some, it was the first time they'd been back in a classroom in a long time. One of the program directors, Hala Helmy, pointed out the context that made this so meaningful. "Women [in Egypt] have so often been suppressed," she said. "In the old ages, women were looked down on as, she's the female, she's at home and she's going to be supported by men." As for empowered negotiation, forget it. "Because she's a woman," Helmy said, "she's not supposed to be speaking up for what she wants, or what she deserves."

To break out of that story, then, was huge for these women. Some were compelled to create a new narrative because their husbands had left them with children but without means to support the family. One student had inherited a business from her husband after he passed away. His family was unsupportive—financially and otherwise—and she simply *had* to take over the business and learn to run it in order to support her children.

My colleagues and I quickly established a sense of community and trust, something we do in every class but which was particularly important in the male-dominated culture. We talked a lot about letting go of the labels placed on them, breaking down hierarchical expectations, and allowing them to open up to who they were as individuals. The staff saw our role as providing a container, holding sacred a space where the women could find and then tell their individual, authentic stories. The experience remains with me as a testament to negotiation's importance in our journey of self-discovery.

"But I'm not a liar": Negotiation as a story of morality

In an exercise I use in class, one student must sell a rare bottle of wine to another. The seller has information indicating that the bottle could be sold for a minimum of $400 before taking a loss, and as much as $1,000. A student named Diane offered to sell the bottle for just $400 right out of the gate. "Why did you set your goal there?" I asked. "You could have reasonably asked for $800 or more."

"But I'm not a liar," she said.

"No," I agreed. "And neither am I."

"There's no data to justify $800," she said.

There actually *was* data to support the $800 goal and even a $1,000 goal—the wine had gone up in value steadily over a period of years, and if you extrapolated the *rate* of growth to the present day, actually $1,000 was a totally reasonable expectation. But before I showed her, I pressed, "Where is your data point for $400? Where is your proof for that number? Because I can show you proof for mine."

Flustered, Diane said, "If I ask for $400, I don't lose money and I'm not cheating anyone."

She was telling a story about the worth of the bottle (and possibly her own) that sold it short. She feared being "bad." I rarely hear someone directly label negotiation this way, and I have to confess that when Diane said, "But I'm not a liar," my hackles rose a little bit and my first instinct was to feel defensive. I *teach* this stuff, and still I had to remind myself that I wasn't out of line in my ask, that I wasn't being dishonest. What Diane verbalized has emotional resonance for so many of us, and there are a thousand subtle societal reasons why. Moralizing the way Diane did can act as a shield to hide what's really going on. We may be self-sabotaging for not asking what we're worth; maybe we don't think we deserve what we're asking for, but it's much easier to say, "I'm not a liar," than to acknowledge that we lack confidence.

I've encountered countless people whose default strategy is to pick a minimal number they can live with and proclaim that it's not negotiable. They'll say things like, "I didn't make the best deal, but I skipped the bargaining. I feel like a human being and I don't care." Think about this statement for a minute: Bargaining, by this view of the world, undercuts your humanity.

Jennifer, a graphic designer, was in business with three other women and they were all close. For the first year or so of the business, they didn't have to negotiate with one another over anything very significant; they all had their own clients and worked independently. Then a client asked them to do a project that they needed to work on collectively. Though they broke up tasks for the project, they didn't discuss how they would split the fee among them at the outset. (Their first mistake, obviously.) Jennifer's partner Laura did the bulk of the work, but Jennifer did a lot, too—more than anyone had initially intended because the project got more complicated. When the payment for the project came in, the partner who handled the finances said she was giving 90 percent of it to Laura and splitting the remaining 10 percent among the other three partners. Jennifer thought it was unfair and said so. "Man, did that set off a firestorm of judgment!" Jennifer told me. "They said things like 'This isn't what our culture is about' and 'We all do things uncompensated to help the company.' I was made to feel like I was being greedy for asking for what I felt I deserved. That there was something morally wrong with saying something was unfair." Jennifer did not take this feedback lightly. "I felt like a bad human being if I ever brought money up." When she brought it up another time, one of her partners said, "It makes me trust you less when you begin every conversation with money."

For years afterward, Jennifer avoided negotiating with her partners. But her feelings festered. Jennifer's resentment grew as she felt she couldn't call out any financial concerns or discrepancies. "I was seriously tormented about this situation, and spent so many nights awake trying to reconcile two things: that I felt I was being treated unfairly, and that I was greedy and selfish for thinking that." Jennifer's predicament was multilayered, but as a first step, she needed to sit more solidly in her own awareness that talking about money, that advocating for herself, **was not bad**. It did not make her a bad person. Now, in her partners' view, it did, and she needed to digest that so that she could approach them in the right way. I'll come back to this fraught issue—the *how* of the ask—in Chapter 4.

Jennifer is hardly alone in her struggle. Another entrepreneur came to see me for advice after she'd asked for 360 feedback from her team. Nearly everyone had said, "She's smart," and "she's nice," but then almost all of the women wrote, *She needs to leave her corporate attitude behind. It's all about money with her, and that's not the culture of our company.* None of the men made this comment. "What's going on?" she asked. "Are women harder on each other, or what?"

The answer is yes, sometimes. Women are harder on each other when we go against our expected gender roles. When we see other women act in ways that we don't feel we can, even though we may want to, our inclination is to punish them.

There are reasons people have come to see negotiation as morally loaded, and that's because many negotiators *do* behave badly. My student Michelle used to work as a litigator for a big firm in New York City, and her experiences reinforced ideas about how strong negotiators fit a certain profile. "Part of the game was to show how tough you could be," she said. "There was a lot of intimidation, posturing, flexing." The message she got in her early career was that negotiation "was serious, it was aggressive, it was zero-sum thinking, it was competitive." If that was what effective negotiation was, she wanted no part of it.

In response, Michelle's approach to negotiation had always been one of trying to work things out, of making other people happy, with a strong focus on not coming across badly. "There was a politeness factor to my approach," she said, "a shame factor, a concern about not coming off as greedy or unreasonable or just bad."

But when Michelle left litigation and joined her family jewelry business, she had to scrap every tale she had told herself about negotiation. If she equated setting a high goal with low professionalism, then she wouldn't succeed in the business. She had to learn to give herself permission to make an ask, and to feel confident that it didn't make her a bad person. "I'm more comfortable saying, 'Here are my needs and here's what I want, and I'm not going to apologize for it.' I can be pleasant and human about the exchange. I don't have to be an asshole. But I don't have to back down, either."

This terrain is really complex, in part because it can be so subtle. It takes a lot of self-awareness to recognize when you're spinning negotiation into a morality tale. Listen to your inner monologue and pick out its themes. I started this book by explaining that we negotiate every day, so start to notice those incidents. Do you feel like a jerk when you negotiate with someone? Why? Do you feel tough (in a good way) when you negotiate? Why? The judgment you do or don't put on negotiation is intensely personal, just as your negotiation style must be. Start finding your way by paying attention.

It's our choice to make

In the second year of the Trump administration, I taught a class of undergraduates at Wharton that shook me. I've been teaching negotiation for fifteen years, and although no year is the same, this class was markedly different. Like many of my undergraduate classes, this one had tremendous diversity in terms of gender, age, race, ethnicity, religion, and life experience. But confidence in negotiation was distinctly lower than I'd seen in years prior.

Typically, I focus the first class on goal setting, on the stories we tell ourselves and why they're so important, and then move on in the next class. Not so in this class. Whenever we unpacked and examined an exercise and the students' results, I'd ask questions about why they set their goals so low, and we'd be back right where we were in the first class. One student, for instance, said that he had set an aspirational goal, but when he began negotiating with his partner, he lacked the desire to ask for what he wanted. Essentially, he was never convinced that he had the right number in the first place, perhaps because he thought his goal was too lofty. I had variations of this conversation all semester; these students lacked self-confidence because they simply couldn't change their story. Stepping back, I thought I understood why. The fractious nature of our society and our world more broadly—where we see more open, obvious discord, and a hyper lack of civility—affects all of us in our day-to-day lives. We can't underestimate how the general ethos of this climate seeps into our psyche. For the most marginalized and underrepresented populations, this discord may be further internalized, becoming their story.

As a result of the class climate, we spent most of the *semester* on setting aspirational goals that they could believe in and thus potentially achieve. Self-esteem became a running theme. In the final class of the year, when I told them to remember that "You are enough . . . just as you are," half the class (and their professor) was teary. I can't say that the political climate was solely responsible for the class's difficulty setting aspirational goals, but I believe it played a huge role. I've seen this play out often in my classes at Wharton where young, high-achieving adults carry what appears to be the weight and burden of the world on their shoulders. Their stories are that their parents risked everything for them to be where they are, so they need to make sure they succeed, or that their peers already have their entire lives planned out, so they must do so as well. Compounded with all that's going on in our world, the issues raised in my class take on a new importance. It's no wonder emotions run high.

To be clear, people feeling inferior because of their race or ethnicity isn't new, it's just much worse than I've ever seen it. Words matter and cut to a core of insecurity that has long been simmering. As Wes Moore, the African American activist and writer, told Oprah Winfrey, "There's a common narrative that we don't belong in a certain place. An imposter syndrome . . . You're just waiting for someone to tap you on the shoulder and say, 'What are you doing here?'" Wes recounted how with every one of his accomplishments, from becoming a decorated veteran to earning a Rhodes scholarship, he thought he wasn't supposed to be there. It's true that the originators of the Rhodes scholarship likely never intended for an African

American to receive it, and that's a narrative he could have held on to. But instead, Wes thought of how many people he had never met had worked their butts off, risked their lives, and kept their hope up because of the *idea* of him. *This* is the story Wes needed to tell. "We are never in a room we don't belong in," he said. "And we have to have confidence that we belong there, and not just as wallpaper."

I've had students tell me that I am the story they remember to tell themselves because I'm a woman of color standing at the head of their classroom. It feels weird to hear this, because I still struggle with self-doubt myself and wonder what in the heck they're seeing. But I also get it. For women like my student Sarah Farzam, who is Iranian, Mexican, and Jewish, who grew up playing with Barbie dolls that never looked like her, who read books and watched shows with characters that never looked like her, seeing an Iranian woman in a position of power matters. Some of my students see me as a woman of color, and others just see a woman, and that's enough. For my part, I've looked up to women like Oprah, Madeleine Albright, and Serena Williams. It's not that I aspire to *be* them, but seeing them be the "first"—seeing them, period—inspires me. If they can break through, why can't we all if we try hard enough? It becomes easier to tell myself a better story. And if I think of this story often enough, I am exercising that muscle of self-confidence to the point that it just kicks in automatically. As a workout fanatic, I love this analogy because there comes a point with every workout regimen where you don't have to think so hard about the muscles you've been developing. Instead, the workout starts and you just *go*.

Research from positive psychology tells us that the more positive our narrative, the better our results. The wisdom in positivity goes back much further, though. In an old Cherokee teaching, a grandfather tells his grandson that he has two wolves living inside him, fighting viciously: one that embodies everything evil within him—like envy, pride, and ego; and one that embodies everything good—like joy, generosity, and compassion. A similar fight, he says, goes on inside every person. When the grandson asks, "Which will win?" the grandfather answers, "The one you feed." Where we choose to focus our energy matters. Which wolf we choose to feed has enormous impact on our sense of self-worth and our ability to negotiate with the world that surrounds us.

CHAPTER 2

when we undercut ourselves to please others

n a classic episode of *The Office*, Dunder Mifflin regional manager and lovable narcissist Michael Scott accidentally hits an employee, Meredith, with his car. Her refusal to instantly forgive him becomes Michael's obsession. Michael tells the camera, "Do I need to be liked? Absolutely not. I like to be liked. I enjoy being liked. I have to be liked. But it's not like this compulsive need to be liked . . . like my need to be praised."

Of course, what makes satire so funny in the first place is that it amplifies what we know is within us, in some form. Everyone wants to be liked. But unchecked, this desire also gets us into trouble, as we give away our power without recognizing that's what we're doing. Those who do this as a matter of course are often called *pleasers*.

Emily is a quintessential pleaser. Years ago, when she and her new husband bought their first used car together, the negotiation process was laborious. Emily's husband was in law school and particularly earnest about negotiating. The salesman, Steve, was growing impatient. He made a big deal out of calling his girlfriend to tell her he would be late for their dinner date. He explained the finer points of his romantic life to Emily while her husband pushed for a deal on the last $1,000. When Steve sighed and made a move to call his girlfriend again and push their dinner date back even further, Emily intervened. She told her husband he should let the last of it go—that Steve's girlfriend was waiting for him. Though this happened fifteen years ago, Emily's husband still insists he buy their cars without Emily present so she can't negotiate against him.

The pleaser hates conflict and avoids it at any cost. If someone takes the last swig out of the office coffeepot, the pleaser who comes up behind him makes a fresh pot. It's not his turn—the guy who took the last cup should do it—but it's not worth the fight. He just doesn't want to deal with the headache of it all. But he doesn't see that there's a cost to his making the coffee, too: He's pissed. Why is *he* always the one to refill the pot? The truth is, by swallowing his ask, by not engaging in negotiation, he is choosing to give away his power.

Or consider the pleaser as a parent. She may not let the tendency show at the office, but when she gets home, she feels so guilty about working so much (or being divorced, or enrolling the kid in tutoring . . . pick your guilt!) that when the kid asks for a second bowl of ice cream, the parent says yes. She doesn't want any conflict, she just wants to enjoy her child for a bit. So when the kid begs to stay up late, again she says yes. When the kid talks back to her, she lets it go. There is little to no negotiation, just acquiescence. In no time, the parent's power is gone.

Although the domestic sphere is common stomping grounds for pleasers, they are found everywhere. And though you may think of pleasers as predominantly female, that's not so. Greg, for instance, had ten years of work experience behind him when he took my executive MBA class. For the rare-wine exercise I wrote about in the last chapter, Greg played the dealer who needed to sell the bottle. His character was planning to retire soon, so he wasn't necessarily looking to develop a relationship with the buyer—just to sell the bottle for as much as possible. Greg looked at the data and determined he could reasonably ask $800, so he set his goal there. Recall that the bottom line, or lowest price before taking a loss, was $400. The buyer's opening offer was $250. So Greg said he could take $500 for it, they agreed, and the deal was done in minutes.

When we debriefed, Greg saw that in many other groups, the seller got $600, $700, and even $800 for the same bottle of wine. When I asked him why he moved away from his goal of $800 so quickly, he said, "It was hard for me to keep relationships out of it." At this point in the term, my students had gotten to know one another well. Greg was a really likable guy and popular with the other students. Reputations form quickly in a class like this—everyone expected Greg to be affable, and so he was. "When the buyer came in so low," he explained of his classmate, who he was friendly with, "I figured there was no way she could pay my goal price." As we unpacked it further, he explained that he'd wanted to minimize the gap between his goal and the buyer's opening offer and avoid the back-and-forth. "I didn't want to appear unreasonable," he said.

Relationships are important, I agree. But Greg was giving away his power—the perceived value of his rare asset—when he could have maintained a friendly rapport *and* gotten more for the wine. Almost without fail, I can tell the pleasers in the classroom from this wine exercise: They always sell the bottle quickly and for less.

There's a confluence of reasons for this: First, because they can't wrap their heads around the true value of the wine, even though there is data to support that story, as I discussed in Chapter 1. Greg knew that the wine was of a rare vintage, for instance. He knew that other dealers had sold the same vintage for $600 and $700 in previous years, and that the value increased each year. This is why he set his goal at $800 in the first place. But he didn't bring any of those details up with his partner. He didn't fully internalize these details and grasp that he had an incredible asset in his possession.

Second, pleasers want to get the deal done and ensure that everyone is happy. In Greg's case, he not only liked his classmate and wanted her to continue liking him, but I suspect that he also felt he needed to please *me*. He hadn't gotten a deal in the previous two class sessions and wanted to come out of this negotiation able to tell me he closed it.

In this chapter, I cover the many forms of the pleaser. Pleasers can be chefs, CEOs, and professional athletes—there's no one stereotype that fits. Likewise, pleasers can be gruff, they can be stoic, they can be so standoffish that you would never peg them as a pleaser. And yet they are. Most people would never guess that I'm a pleaser. I come across as a little removed, at least at first. But though I don't have kids, I have a strong maternal instinct that I attribute to my Iranian heritage. Iranians are masters of hospitality, who subscribe to a mantra that "Your comfort is my comfort." I always want things to be okay for others, though it comes less from a need to be liked and more from a need for everything to be in balance, for everyone around me to be happy.

Even if you are not a pleaser yourself, you need to understand the mentality, as the likelihood is that you are close to someone who is—maybe your spouse, your daughter, your colleague, or your best friend, and it's important to recognize when they are biting back an ask. I cover what fear of *no*—saying it and hearing it—has to do with a need to be liked, and how a discomfort with silence plays into an inclination to give away our power. I address the costs of the pleaser mentality gone awry—a cost that looks a lot like resentment—and how pleasers particularly wrestle with being stuck in situations where they recognize they can't please everyone.

"I wanted all to be fine and well in the world"

One day after a class I gave to entrepreneurs, I noticed a student, Liz, lingering. I took my time packing up my bag, and when we were the only two people left in the classroom, she asked if we could talk. Liz was impressive in every way. She'd been an executive at a large company for years before deciding to start her own business. Now that business was thriving. Liz already had a reputation in class for being smart, confident, and tough yet fair. She looked a little shaken, though, and I suggested we go out for a cup of coffee to discuss whatever was on her mind.

"Class today was pretty intense for me," she said when we were situated at a nearby café. I thought back over that day's seminar. We'd talked quite a bit about the tendency so many have to give away their power to please others. It was a lively discussion, but Liz hadn't contributed much. In fact, she'd been uncommonly quiet.

"I seem really together and everything," she said. "And I guess I am—now. But there's some stuff in my past that I hadn't really worked through, and class today brought it up for me."

She explained that when she'd joined the large organization where she worked before becoming an entrepreneur, she hadn't felt worthy of it. "I would often think, *Why am I here? This job is too big for me and it's only a matter of time before they realize it.* I was overly tough on myself and thought I needed to perform at a crazy level. I had a terrible case of imposter syndrome."

Her boss at the organization was supportive and looked for ways to empower her, repeatedly telling Liz, "You've got this." "I got along really well with him in the beginning," she explained. "We were completely aligned—it was us against the world, and we bonded over our shared purpose. We spent a lot of time together and became good friends. All along, I grew more confident in the work I was doing. But as time went on, I started noticing things about my boss that I didn't like. I didn't like the way he talked about other people. I didn't like the strategies he used when working with others, which struck me as manipulative. He said inappropriate things to me about my appearance because he had gotten so comfortable with me. I didn't call him out on his behavior, but I put distance between us. I still did my work to the same level as always, but I avoided spending as much time with him."

Liz's boss noticed. After a work event, when Liz accepted a ride home from a colleague, he was pissed. He said, "Don't you know what it looks like if you drive away with him?" But it made no sense, Liz emphasized, because his alternative solution was that he would take her home. If optics were the issue, that would look just as bad. So Liz shrugged off his concern. "Soon I noticed that I started being left out of meetings. It didn't matter much to me at first, because I trusted my boss's intentions, and I was neck-deep in work anyway so I was happy to miss a meeting or two. But as time went on, I had an unsettled feeling."

Liz didn't take her concerns to anyone else at the company. "I wanted all to be fine and well in the world," she said. "I wanted everyone—even my boss, from whom I now kept my distance—to be okay, and I suppose I wanted to protect him. So I ignored my instincts. I doubled down on the work I was doing, focusing on the fact that it was going really well. I was getting exceptional results."

Soon after, her boss took her out for dinner and said, "Liz, it looks like you're not enjoying your job anymore. We used to spend more time together, but it seems like you don't have time for me anymore. We don't communicate the way we once did."

Naturally, Liz wondered what that had to do with her enjoying her job. But she didn't say that. Instead she said, "No, I love what I'm doing. I love this work."

The next week, she said, she went into his office for her scheduled review. He closed the door and said, "This isn't working anymore."

Liz's voice was soft when she got to this part of the story and I could tell she was fighting back tears. "It's an understatement to say I was flabbergasted," she said. "I was not only meeting my goals but, in many ways, exceeding expectations. The president of the company had taken the time to praise me during my last meeting with him. My team was efficient and productive, and we all worked really hard. I didn't know what was happening, or, at least in that moment, why. I was shaking. I left the building without even saying good-bye to my team.

"Almost immediately afterward, I was furious with myself. Why hadn't I taken the red flags seriously? Why had I shrugged off the encounter at our dinner, when it was clear I wasn't being evaluated fairly?"

Liz learned that her boss left shortly thereafter, for reasons she was never quite clear on. But it didn't change what had happened. Her career at that organization was through.

"In the months and years that followed," she said, "it was painful for me to think about that job and the way I left. In fact, I was a wreck about it. I've only told a handful of people the story. But today brought it all up for me."

I squeezed her hand and we sat quietly together for a while. I didn't feel she needed me to say anything but rather just needed to be heard. I appreciated the moment of reflection, as it allowed me to sort through my own emotions about what she'd said. That this confident, amazing woman could have doubted herself at the job in the first place was hard to believe. She had given away her power, and there was no way I could spin the story otherwise, nor was she looking for me to. What happened to her happens to women all the time—their desire for everything to be okay for everyone else outweighed their desire for everything to be okay for *themselves*. And it happens almost instinctually, such that they give away all of their power before they realize it. All I could say to Liz was that I was sorry it had happened. And then I said she could be sure it would not happen to her again.

Missing the moment to negotiate

Needing to be liked isn't something you would guess of a company founder, sales guy, and tough-seeming New Yorker like James. But people are complicated, and the desire to please runs deep and defies stereotypes. (I also never would have guessed that outside of work James is a minister, which he is!) Last year he had a huge project for an internet company at Madison Square Garden that needed to be done in a short time frame. "I tried to anticipate everything, but in this case I knew that there was a possibility of things not getting done on the timeline of the client wanting it to get done," he said. But, eager to please, he didn't raise his concerns with their timetable, and he didn't say no. And indeed, the schedule started to slip. "There were a lot of factors beyond my control," James said. "I was relying on other vendors, relying on the City of New York. The customer was calling me and saying, 'What's happening? When is this going to change?' I kept saying, 'It's okay—we'll get there,' but I didn't have control of it—not really. I started to shut down."

In the end, the project was completed, albeit a few days late. The client didn't care about the delay and was thrilled with the result. But the whole ordeal was incredibly stressful for James. "I just wanted to solve it, make everyone happy so I could move on. . . . If I could do it all over again, I would have been more straightforward with the customer from the beginning. I would have said, 'I can do this, it's possible, but just be aware that there are things outside of my control and it might not happen.' I wish I'd been more confident about being up front with them, instead of feeling I didn't want to disappoint them."

It's notable that, just as with Liz's quick departure from the company she loved, the tendency to please is almost reflexive. Great care needs to be taken to acknowledge that you are in a negotiation at all. Sometimes we don't even realize that there are opportunities for us to counter with a solution that works for us because we are so used to just going along. Pleasers, in other words, can completely miss their moment to negotiate.

Dylan Reim, a former student of mine, didn't recognize his predisposition to go along until an in-class exercise wherein he played the part of someone who had received an offer from a start-up. His task was to negotiate the offer's terms with the HR director. "When I went into that," he said, "I felt like I was still interviewing. Even though this person and I had never met before, I thought, *I can't have them thinking I'm anything less than committed to this position. This is not a place where I get to negotiate.*" In other words, to his mind, negotiating at all would come off badly. As we discussed in the debrief, though, the exercise was not an interview, it was a negotiation. He had already been chosen. The company had said that they wanted him as much as he wanted to be there. "Remembering that gives you so much emotional leverage," he said. "You just need to remind yourself that you see them exactly the way they see you." In other words, sure, you like them, but *they like you, too!* Asking for more will not change that. Miss the moment too often, and you're looking at a significant wage gap between those who ask and those who didn't realize that they could.

Former NFL star and former college football coach Hardy Nickerson remembered when he was first hired as a coach with the Tampa Bay Buccaneers. Up to that point, his role had been that of a player, and he had agents taking care of him. He'd never had to negotiate for himself. Added to that was the fact that he really wanted this job. His first impulse when the team told him what they were going to pay him was to think, "Okay, I guess that's my salary." But then he recalled what he learned in my negotiations course. He now knew his initial thought was reflexive, borne out of a desire to go along to get along. "It occurred to me, *wait, no—this is a negotiation*," he said. "So I said, 'What if you paid me such-and-such?'"

We don't stop to think what would happen if we *don't* just go along. And although Hardy's experience shows that this happens to both men and women, there is also a gender element that can't be ignored here. In one of the most striking studies I've ever seen on the issue, subjects were told that they would be observed playing a word game and paid between $3 and $10. After the game, the experimenter said, "Here's $3. Is $3 okay?" The men's requests for more money exceeded the women's by *nine to one*.

There's a personality trait called *sociotropy*, more common in women, wherein a person cares a great deal about interpersonal relationships and being accepted by others. People with this personality trait will be overly nurturing, even to strangers. Studies show a correlation between sociotropy and eating more around others, and eating higher-calorie foods, because the sociotropic individual is so inclined to induce feelings of pleasure and not guilt in whomever they're with.

A friend of mine who is sociotropic recently traveled to France, where her pleaser inclinations shone brightly. The French, in general, do not tend to be overly welcoming, and may even see American friendliness as inauthentic. Even knowing this, my friend constantly squirmed under what she perceived to be French disapproval of her every move or utterance. One evening she was paying the check at a restaurant, and when the waiter came over with a credit card reader, he asked her how much of a tip she would like to leave: 10, 15, or 20 percent? My friend knew that it's not customary to tip for service in France but rather to leave a euro or two if you have them handy. But she was such a reflexive pleaser that she didn't want to disappoint or feel awkward around this stranger whom she would never see again. He ended up getting a much healthier tip than he should have.

Julia is a management consultant and, like James, she has struggled with that moment when a client makes an ask, and you want more than anything to say yes in order to make them happy. The consultant world is very high-stakes; clients pay top dollar for services like Julia's, and they expect a lot in return. "There are always moments when you're in information overload," she said, "and the impulse in those moments is to squander opportunity to hold your ground. I could be in a room with my consulting team and have my client on the phone telling me, 'We need this kind of deliverable and your deliverable isn't getting it right now.'" You may not realize it, but this is a negotiation. It's subtle, but it is. "They have an ask," said Julia, "and your response could impact what you have to do . . . sometimes, the information overload makes it impossible to real-time process." The natural instinct of the pleaser in this situation is to agree to whatever will make the client happy—or at least, happier. The trap is set. The pleaser says yes even though she's unsure she can deliver what they're asking. And then kills herself to please again.

Julia will say, "Let me think about that and get back to you." Or, if she's able to identify what it is about the client's ask that concerns her, she'll say, "Here's what's going on in my head, and here are my concerns." She'll be open about her lack of confidence in getting them what they want. "I'll tell them I'm worried about the time my team has. I'll share a bit more. I'll explain that the team has focused on this other list of priorities, and engage the client in a discussion around what is actually most important to tackle—people are reasonable, and will accept that there are trade-offs." Pushing aside her desire to please and sharing her concerns is far better than attesting that she can do it but feeling terror on the inside.

Time management coach Elizabeth Grace Saunders writes about how a big piece of the boundaries problem is that people set up unrealistic expectations for how their role is defined. For instance, say you're a manager and you always keep your door open when you're not in meetings, because you feel that accessibility is part and parcel of being a good manager. The problem is, that means that you never get the work that requires quiet done during work hours, and so you end up doing that work during family time. Saunders argues that the solution is redefining what it means to be a good manager. Sure, a good manager is reasonably accessible, but a good manager also shows how important it is to focus on high-priority work. "In instances like this," she says of the manager who won't close her door, "you've set up strict rules about what someone in a role should or shouldn't do; but in fact, these rules are negotiable."

For pleasers who struggle with *no*, then, a few things are helpful to keep in mind: (1) Watch your reflexive instincts. It's too easy if you're energetic and generally a "can-do" kind of a person to say yes and miss the negotiation altogether; and (2) remember that saying yes to one thing might well be saying no to another. Saying yes to a demanding client at work means more pressure and less sleep; saying yes when the French waiter asks if you want to leave a big tip means you don't have enough budgeted to take your kid out for a special dessert afterward. Something has to give, and that something might be your critical self-care, so knowing that can help you be more strategic about what you say yes to. And (3) check whether your reason for the yes is intertwined with an unrealistic definition of your role. Don't blindly accept this definition—question it. This is harder than it may seem, because often just the promise of a business relationship is enough to make us overcommit.

Resentment: The hidden danger for the pleaser

Women are particularly prone to be pleasers, but it may surprise you that I have seen this with pro football players, too. There is a common dynamic in which NFL players—and professional athletes in general—have friends and family around them who always lean on them for money. When this happens, the athletes feel like they can't say no because they'll appear ungrateful for their good fortune, or greedy, or perceived as if they're turning their backs on those who supported them before they "made it." So they say yes, and yes, and yes, until they become resentful.

When Hardy Nickerson was chosen as a fifth-round draft pick

for the Pittsburgh Steelers back in 1987, the newspapers reported that he'd signed for a quarter of a million dollars (which, by today's standards, is laughably low for a fifth-round pick). His extended family thought they'd hit the jackpot—that they would no longer have to work, that Hardy could pay off their car payments and pick up random expenses. But no one did the math—it was a multiyear contract, so he made $75,000 a year before taxes. Still, he said, it was good money and he helped wherever he could. Things changed when he had children of his own and his financial focus changed to providing for them. "Telling people no is hard," he said. "You think, 'They were with me when I wasn't so-and-so,' which makes it difficult. But I've had to tell my mother no. I had to tell my father no." He said it created a lot of resentment all around, but now he has a better perspective on it. He transitioned to the role of coach—for high school, college, and the NFL—and has mentored dozens of young players. "What I try to tell people—especially those guys who are first-generation anything," he said, "is that you can help those around you but you have to understand where you're at and to what extent you can help them. And you have to ask, is that help something that's going to create a line of more handouts down the road, or it is something that's going to help them grow from that help and produce something from the help?" Otherwise, he said, players can get to a point where they feel like a human ATM.

Although many athletes initially feel good about being in a position to help the people who helped them in some way before they became professional athletes, they will at some point, sooner than later, feel resentful. *Why does everyone think that I have endless resources? I feel like they're taking advantage of this situation.* (Incidentally, it's a positive when they realize it. Sometimes they never do and run into financial challenges as a result.) The players end up removing themselves from relationships instead of just confronting-ing what's making them uncomfortable. When asked why these relationships have gone sour, they externalize it. "So-and-so was taking advantage of me." I push back. "Did you ever say no? Did you ever set boundaries?" Others can't know what we want if we don't say it, and this is true whether it's about refilling the coffeepot, being treated badly by a boss, or getting hit up constantly for money.

I think of what these athletes experience as the "friends and family syndrome," and I see it all the time with entrepreneurs who have a service business. A proprietor of a coffee shop gives everyone he's ever met a discount. The graphic designer is asked to make everyone's websites or business cards and never says no. These entre-preneurs don't want to hurt their relationship with the person asking. But if they don't say no, if they don't draw a boundary, they're hurting the relationship anyway because they're chipping away at it with a little hammer called resentment. They don't see that they can say no and still preserve the relationship.

When you set a boundary, you are putting focus on yourself and your needs, but that doesn't mean you're not looking out for others' needs as well. "I would love to design the logo for your daughter's school auction," the graphic designer might say to his cousin, "be-cause you're family and of course I want to help this good cause. There are a lot of causes I want to help with. But if I did that, I wouldn't have time to finish my paid work and keep a thriving busi-ness." How you explain your position will vary because so will the boundaries. The only hard-and-fast rule: Know what you're willing to do for others without putting yourself in a bad spot or fostering resentment. What can you afford? What's your budget? How often will you do it? Is there a particular category you will always cover if you can, versus the never-ending ask? For instance, I've advised

NFL players to say things to their family and friends such as, "I will cover educational or medical expenses to the point I can, but that's all I can do."

Boundaries like these are hard to set in office settings, too, where, as in the case of the manager who never closes his door, people negotiate against themselves without even recognizing it. Sheryl, for example, is a professor of economics at a university. She is a numbers person, so she is all about the most probable outcomes and labor economics. She is highly accomplished, a sought-after power player, and she knows it. So she negotiated a healthy raise for herself about a year ago. A few months later, she was asked to lead up the department's administrative team—a two-year, time-consuming extra commitment that did not come with extra compensation. Sheryl figured she should do it—she had just gotten this big raise and wanted to be seen as a team player. Then another professor had to take a leave of absence and asked Sheryl to take over his class. Sheryl was told it would just be five classes, and that he'd return the favor the following year, so she agreed. Again, she wanted to be seen as a team player, and she knew that because of her raise, she was being compensated more than anyone else in the department. As it turned out, her colleague was going to miss ten classes, not five. And Sheryl would also have to do additional office hours and much more grading than she'd originally understood.

Sheryl felt stuck. She swallowed her desire to renegotiate and missed her moment. Even though she has tenure, and her job is in no way at risk, she felt she had to please her department heads and accommodate this professor. Now she is frustrated, and angry at most everyone else in her department. She feels overworked and underappreciated. Her husband isn't too happy about the situation, either, as she is now away from home teaching most nights, putting more burden on him to take care of the kids. Sheryl had done a great job knowing her worth and telling herself the right story when she negotiated her raise. But then her pleaser instinct kicked in, and she lost most of what she'd gained.

The cost of resentment like Sheryl's is no small matter. She put herself last, thinking it noble, or the right thing to do. I see this pitfall constantly with entrepreneurs who don't see the trade-offs they're really making. In some cases, it leads to burnout, or divorce, or family feuds. It leads to leaving a job you might love. The pleaser isn't likely to think about these costs, believing she can handle it. That's what makes this habit so dangerous. And so ironic, because it's a desire to avoid making waves that causes pleasers to say yes in the first place.

Although these are all professional examples, personal examples are everywhere. When my friend Maria's second child was an infant and she was tired more often than not, whenever her husband asked if she'd be solo with the kids so he could meet friends or go on a camping trip, she automatically said yes. She wanted him to be happy, and she'd always said "Go for it" whenever he'd asked before. But then she found herself more and more resentful every time he came home. It wasn't his fault he'd gone—she'd told him to. But she'd done so reflexively. In time, she learned not to respond right away when he asked. She still wanted to say yes—and she often would—but she knew she needed to take a moment to really think through whether she had the bandwidth to handle the kids by herself. She would ask herself, "If I say yes, am I going to resent him when he comes home?" If the answer was yes, then they would think of another option together, whether it was getting a babysitter or making sure that she had part of that day to herself, too.

When we care about people, we can feel like saying no will hurt them. We don't want them to feel belittled or rejected, and in Maria's case, she also wanted to maintain the job description she'd set up for herself as an accommodating, easygoing wife. But there's no way around the buildup of anger that happens when you instinctually overpromise.

The fear of *no*

Just as much as they fear saying no, pleasers are afraid of *hearing* no. This fear takes up so much room in our psyche that we don't want to put ourselves in the position where we hear it at all. We either don't ask for what we should, or we rush to fill up a silence that we fear will lead to a negative response. Think of how often we end conversations or emails that contain an ask with "If it doesn't work for you, I understand," or "This is of course negotiable." Why? Why do we immediately offer an easy out? Because we've already told ourselves they'll come back and say no, and we're so afraid of that word that cushioning it makes it less scary. When people recognize how often they do this unthinkingly, it's jarring. A friend of mine told me she didn't realize she had this tendency until she was helping her young daughter craft an email "ask" for a school fund-raiser and encouraged her to end it with, "I totally understand if this doesn't work." We coach backing off before we coach for courage.

One average guy, a freelance IT specialist named Jason Comely, made a game out of hearing no when he realized that his fear of it was holding him back. He decided that he needed to get used to hearing it. He aimed to get rejected every single day, so he would ask strangers for things he pretty much knew they'd reject—like a ride across town, or a discount on something he hadn't yet purchased. The desensitization was so empowering for him that he made a card game out of it called Rejection Therapy. "You're going to feel great afterward," he told NPR about getting intentionally rejected. "You're going to feel like, 'Wow. I disobeyed fear.'" I really like the idea of this game, though dramatic immersion like that isn't for everyone. I'm deathly afraid of snakes, but the last thing that would help me get over it would be to be surrounded by the nasty creatures. Just the image is enough to give me a heart attack. The point, though, isn't whether desensitization is the most effective way to get over a fear of no, but that the word *no* is so frightening and paralyzing for so many people that they are driven to somehow, some way loosen its power over them.

I spend an inordinate amount of time with my students talking about this fear of hearing no, but my approach is less about desensitization and more about looking at the entire exchange differently. Instead of seeing *no* as rejection, see it as a piece of information in a larger conversation. What other information can you get from that *no*? Where can it take you?

Undeniably, some *no*s just suck. If you get rejected from a grant or a job, for instance, and you get a form letter telling you so, it's tempting to just turn away from the no because it's painful. But I coach people to summon the confidence to turn into it instead. It's still information. If the rejector is willing, you could try to find out why you were rejected, so that you can do better next time. Granted, it's not comfortable, but in the words of the great Wayne Gretzky, "You'll always miss 100 percent of the shots you don't take."

This is very different from the telemarketer's way of not taking no for an answer. Usually working from a script, they don't take the conversation further, they don't ask questions, and they won't let you off the phone. As a result you feel you haven't been listened to. That's enough to make anyone crazy. What I'm recommending is very different and is all about being inquisitive and not being afraid to stay in the conversation.

Entrepreneurs have their own version of the Rejection Therapy game, as often getting funding and customers requires no after no after no. They have to learn from those *nos*, or they'll never get off the ground. Sebastian Jackson was told no three times by Wayne State University before they agreed to let him open a barbershop on campus. "That first no was tough because I did hear it as no," he said. "But I was encouraged to go back to figure out why I was told no. That was a lightbulb moment for me." His request for a meeting to learn *why* he was told no was also rejected, though. So he found someone internally at Wayne State who understood how the university made its business decisions. This person said that the rejection was less about the business model than it was about Sebastian personally, as he'd worked in the previous campus barbershop that had failed. What made Sebastian think he could own a barbershop and succeed? The decision makers weren't convinced he had an answer.

Sebastian set out to solve the problem. He requested letters of recommendation that would bolster what he personally could bring to the business, then submitted them to the university and asked again. Again they said no. This time they told him it was because his business model was shaky. So he went back to the drawing board and made the model more clear. A third time, the university said no, explaining that he didn't have enough money to execute what he wanted to do. Still Sebastian didn't give up. And although he might not have had much money, he did have enough to pay rent on the barbershop space—a space that the university was currently losing money on because it didn't have a tenant. Finally, the university relented. Sebastian had used those *nos* as data and shown that he had the perseverance to succeed. (As a side note, Sebastian's barbershop, The Social Club, is wildly successful. Beyond cutting hair, The Social Club is a social connector and community builder in Detroit, and I'll come back to it later.)

Believe it or not, when you begin to see *no* as a piece of data in a conversation, then when you get an immediate *yes* it doesn't feel as gratifying anymore. *No* gives you the opportunity to go deeper into a conversation, and to know each other better. In fact, a good *no* that gives you more information is more valuable than a bad *yes*.

Discomfort with silence

As Francis Bacon said, "Silence is the sleep that nourishes wisdom." The pleaser should take note, as pleasers tend not to let things just sit when they need to, not to let them breathe. "I hate silence," said my student James. "I feel this angst poke at me, like I need to fill up some empty space because it's uncomfortable. If I give someone a cost and they cringe, my past reaction would be to try to find a way to make them feel better." When you jump in too soon, though, you don't give yourself time to think through a response, and you don't give your counterpart time to let things settle. It takes a lot of confidence to just sit in silence, particularly for entrepreneurs who, one way or another, are always selling. They frequently go to a story of doubt: *Oh no, was it too expensive? Oh no, did I lose this deal?*

"Sometimes things have to take their course," James said. "It can't be solved right away. Sometimes the person on the other side needs time to process things. But trying to come up with a solution, immediately trying to solve the problem, is not always solving the problem." James struggled to put this into practice in his career and had to dig deep to understand why it was so hard for him. "I have this personal thing where I struggle when something is hanging out there and is unresolved. It's hard for me to move on to the next issue. I need to solve it right away if I have a perception that a customer would be angry with me or disappointed with me."

James has made being comfortable with silence a goal, and he actively practices it, just as he actively practices not jumping in to "fix" things right away. "Not reacting quickly . . . has more beneficial outcomes in whatever business scenario I'm in. . . . Maybe instead of lowering the cost I come up with an idea to make the product in a less expensive way. I don't have to cut my cost. I'm giving the customer something at a better price or a better price point. I've found that to be very beneficial in my business life." It's one thing to know that comfort with silence is important, and another matter altogether to actually *be* comfortable with it. Practicing, as James does, helps—but so does feeling confident in your ask. If you know you are on solid ground in whatever it is you're proposing, it's much easier to just let it sit there instead of rushing in to compensate somehow for the fact that you've asked at all.

I personally find that I'm comfortable with silence when I'm sitting in the presence of my counterpart. There's still so much information I'm able to glean—about his posture, the tilt of his head, the subtle expressions on his face. I begin feeling less comfortable with silence as physical distance grows. I don't do well with silence on the phone, but I try not to focus on the dead space. I often try to just kill time on my end by sending an email or looking through my in-box while I wait. Email silence is the most distant, and, for me, the most uncomfortable. If I send a potential client a proposal and suggested fee structure, for instance, and don't hear back right away, I go a little nuts. That's when my storytelling factory starts up big-time, and I start thinking they're stunned by my high fees; I start fearing I'm an imposter and that I most certainly overbid. I squirm and doubt and am generally not a happy person. I do not, however, write back: "Haven't heard from you. Just wanted to check in. I want to make sure you know that what I proposed is completely negotiable." Instead, I have a friend I go to, who knows me well and is very familiar with the ways that my confidence can spin when faced with email silence. He tells me I'm overreacting and assures me that my bid was reasonable. More important, he reminds me of my success and my value to the organization. He brings me back to the place of confidence and authority. It's because of those reminders that I find patience and feel grounded. I sit tight. I wait and trust the process.

Not everyone has a friend perfectly suited for this job, just as not everyone will struggle with email silence. It's hard to give purely prescriptive guidelines because it's all so personal. You have to figure out where your own weak spots are—whether email, in person, or phone, and work on shoring them up in the way that keeps your inner doubter at bay.

You can't please everyone

Now that I'm grown, I can vividly imagine what it must have been like for my parents to leave their home in Iran, to leave their family, and to start over again with a new language and culture. It was undoubtedly terrifying, lonely, and alienating, but what drove them was what drives so many immigrants: the hope for a better future for their children.

As a kid growing up in Massachusetts and New Jersey, I didn't really understand this, or perhaps I didn't want to. What I did understand was that I was two different people. I was Morvarid at home, dutiful and compliant. I spoke Farsi. I was fascinated by sports, by the energy surrounding athletic competition, but was never encouraged to play sports—instead, I did what was expected of me . . . I studied.

Outside of home, I was Mori, spoke English, and wore and did pretty much what I pleased. I'd wait until I got to school to put makeup on, not necessarily because I thought my mom would say I couldn't wear it, but it wouldn't *feel* right to do at home. As I got older, I partied, I dated, and did what every other American kid did. I lived a double life, but that doesn't mean I was rebellious. I never did anything to spite my parents—in fact, I often hid signs of my assimilation from them because I understood that it would disappoint them. I didn't want to cause anyone pain.

When I went away to college, my father expected me to study medicine. And in order to make him happy, I did. I went through college preparing for a medical career, and never once enjoyed the ride. I perpetually swam upstream, trying to excel in courses that I didn't find even remotely interesting. I wanted to take classes in history, economics, and politics and instead took biology, organic chemistry, and physics to meet the requirements of my major. I was living out my father's dream, not mine. When I found the courage to tell him I was conflicted, that I didn't think I wanted to study medicine, we didn't speak again for months. I took the MCAT before I was ready to turn my back on medical school for good. I felt like I had betrayed my parents, who had risked everything by leaving their country so that I could have opportunities. Even now, I still wonder if I'm a disappointment to my parents because I didn't fulfill their dreams for me. But I had to stop living my life to please others, fearing that I would never find personal fulfillment— whatever that meant.

My mom had her own fears, particularly surrounding my personal life. She began to worry as I went through my twenties and thirties without bringing home a nice Iranian boy. Every now and then, she pressured me about getting married and having kids. Meanwhile, unbeknownst to her, I *was* dating, and even became serious about one or two men. But I never let the relationships progress. If a guy wasn't Iranian, I knew that being with him meant risking my relationship with my family. For him to be worth that risk, he had to be perfect. If you've seen *The Big Sick*, you know exactly what I'm talking about. Comedian Kumail Nanjiani complies— on the surface –with his Pakistani parents' wishes but falls in love with a white girl. When she gets sick with a mysterious illness that leaves her in a coma, his double life comes to a head.

My situation came to a head, too, but over something much less dramatic. One particular visit to my parents' house, my mom had a friend over for thinly veiled reasons. This friend had another friend who had an eligible son, and she wanted me to meet him. I was thirty-three, and much too old, by Iranian standards, to be single and childless. But I was too old by *my* standards to have my parents interfere with my love life. I didn't want to even meet this guy, because in my mind, I equated Iranian men with machismo and traditions I wanted to separate myself from. If my parents were setting me up, I knew it would be with a vision of what they wanted, and nothing of what I wanted. I was furious. I turned from the more compliant Dr. Jekyll they were used to into a crazy Mr. Hyde, right in front of my mother's eyes. My family had seen my anger before, but never like that. This is the pleaser's trap: I didn't set boundaries, I wanted to please, and then I flipped out.

I flew back to my home in D.C. and waited a day or two before calling my mom. And as I'd done with my father when I stopped studying medicine, I set a boundary. "Listen," I said, "I have accepted our heritage, and I've done much of what you have wanted me to do. But love? I'm not going to let you guys decide that one for me. That decision is not yours but only mine to make."

My mother was quiet, so I continued. "I'll never say never, but chances are good that whoever I marry is probably not going to be Iranian. I know that's pulling your heart out right now. But I can't bear having these fights anymore. Let me not hurt you with my anger. You need to leave it alone. I will be okay. The man I marry will be wonderful, he just won't be someone you probably expect him to be."

I knew she was upset when we hung up, but I could suddenly breathe more easily—it was like my lungs had found a whole new compartment. I had found the courage to express my authentic self to my mom.

I can't say the fights stopped when my parents accepted that I wasn't going to be a doctor, or when they understood that I would not agree to their setting me up with men. But something very powerful happened. I stopped being angry with my parents. When I found the courage to stop pleasing them, when I gave myself permission to prioritize my integrity and values above all else, I realized that I was living as my authentic self. I just wished I'd done it earlier and during some critical junctures in my life—maybe when I was taking all of those chemistry classes instead of political science, maybe when I was dating a nice guy whom I could have made a future with.

But instead of the continued burden of looking back, teaching has become the opportunity for me to help others, to give them the permission to be who they are and ask for what they want. Their wants and needs are important, and even if they still strive to make others happy (which isn't in and of itself a bad goal!), they first have to find their own satisfaction and negotiate for themselves.

CHAPTER 3

letting scars define us

I never became the doctor my father hoped I would, but I did find public health education and prevention fascinating, which is what led me to HIV outreach work. The business of health care and finding ways to provide access to those in need was something I loved. I decided to apply to business schools and pursue a career in the health care business. As luck would have it, not long after beginning my business school applications, I was offered funding to grow an HIV education program I'd developed. Just like that, I cofounded a health care consulting practice and became one of legions of entrepreneurs struggling to appease doubtful voices—from within and without. My family thought I was crazy. It was one thing not to go to medical school, but to start a company, give up full-time employment, and defer an MBA? What was I thinking? Medicine or a master's degree had appealed to my parents because they were stable professional paths. Entrepreneurship was the polar opposite.

I went for it anyway. Although the company, which I cofounded with my mentor, was initially successful, we ran into trouble when our biggest client didn't renew a contract that we thought was a sure thing. We had counted on that contract and became financially overextended. Our debt appeared insurmountable and the economy simultaneously took a major downturn. My partner felt we needed to let most of our staff go to avoid potential bankruptcy.

I felt very differently. I wanted to continue to keep staff on and worried about their job prospects given the state of the economy. Even with our vendors, I felt a great sense of responsibility to ensure that we stayed on track with our payments; it wasn't their fault that we'd overcommitted. Even if I had to pull money out of my personal accounts, in my mind, we had an obligation to settle our debt. For my partner, who was much older than I was and had decades of business experience, this was just business and not personal. "This is why we are an S corp," he said. "This is why bankruptcy is an option—to protect us in just such a situation."

To me, bankruptcy was synonymous with failure, and I could not tell my family, or others who had been so worried about my starting a business, that the company had failed. Although our business ultimately survived the downturn and we found new clients and large projects, we continued to service our debt for years. Even on more sound financial footing, I found less joy and professional satisfaction from the business—and yet still I felt I had to keep it going.

Nelson Mandela said, "May your choices reflect your hopes, not your fears." It took me a long time to recognize I was letting myself be defined by the scars of my childhood, by this outsized fear of failing. My parents had sacrificed so much in order for me to grow up in the United States, and I did not want to disappoint them.

No one gets through life without scars of one type or another. And most of us let ourselves be defined by them at some point. We have a bad relationship and instead of taking lessons from it and marching onward, we swear off relationships or we become convinced we're only suited for those bad relationships. Or we lose a job we love, and somehow believe it's our doing, so we'd better take what we can get from now on. Or we grow up with a particular set of values that, even though they don't serve us, we can't break free of. Everyone has scars, and when not seen for what they are, they hamper our ability to think clearly and negotiate effectively.

A fighting mind-set

Growing up, Song-I understood a narrow definition of negotiation. In her Korean family, negotiating meant there were winners and there were losers. If you won, the other party went down. Period. "I used to see my family's terms as very black and white—like there's one metric and that's all there is. I would either subvert my desires so as not to fight or get super defensive or angry and go head-to-head. We wouldn't talk, but we'd yell at each other."

As newly arrived immigrants to the United States, she said, they were surrounded by a fighting mind-set all the time. "A lot of people in the immigrant community around me came because they're running away from something like debt or a bad spouse," she said. "There's a lot of pain and stomping over other people to try to win—what, I don't know. Maybe some self-respect or feeling you're better than other people." Her family slept in people's closets for their first months in the States, and Song-I's father worked as a janitor while going to school and also studying to be a pastor. He was generous with people and keen on helping others—and ended up being taken advantage of by others, leaving him with a sinking amount of bad credit, strained family circumstances, and fighting. "I would watch my parents fight about the strain my dad's generosity caused us and think, *You can't be a good person and not get trampled.* That informed what I believed a negotiation can be," she said. "One person benefits and then the other one gets quashed or eliminated or ends up with a sinkhole of debt. . . . I was scared of negotiation. I saw it as a conflict-heavy fight."

When she was an undergrad at Penn, Song-I enrolled in my negotiations class. "My ultimate goal wasn't to be a hard-ass—the reason I wanted to take it was because negotiation made me uncomfortable. I knew I was unhappy and not good at asking for what I wanted. I wanted to face it."

In my class, she had to push against her scars—a message, and a way of being, that she had internalized for twenty years. Instead of a black-and-white framework, she came to see negotiation as problem solving with endless complexities and nuances. And she found she loved it—she loved the process of learning information about other people, and figuring out where their interests overlapped. She also learned that she was naturally very good at it. She was a skilled listener and her classmates respected her.

Song-I had long been taught that Korean women were not expected to ask for what they wanted, let alone fight for it. They should serve others first, themselves last. Intellectually she did not believe that her wants and needs didn't matter, but when it came to the moment of the "ask" it was hard for her to speak up. This became really evident in class. She struggled to advocate for her own needs, but when given the exercise of being a real estate agent for a buyer, she could argue confidently for her client all night long. "That I had the ability to be assertive and fight for things was shocking," she said. "Why couldn't I do that for myself?" Once she saw this, it began to change everything for her. She strove to be informed by her past but not let it dictate her habits.

After the class she went on a trip to Thailand, where she took a baby step into her new mind-set. "As I was setting up a reservation for an airport transfer, the company notified me that it would charge 300 THB (baht). However, the original price that a third party had posted was 250 THB. Now, I realize this may be a no-brainer to some people to claim the original 250, but given my past behavior I'd normally avoid the potential conflict/confrontation and just go with the 300. In the grand scheme of things, a 50-baht difference amounts to ~$1.50 and it wouldn't kill me to stimulate Thailand's economy for the opportunity cost of a pack of gum. However, I decided that I should try growing somewhat of a backbone and at least put it out there that the third party had promised 250 . . . and I got an email saying that 250 would be fine! I know it's not much from an objective point of view, but I had to go through a lot of psychological hurdles to be able to do that."

Song-I's early experiences with negotiation had huge implications, all made through small habits and microdecisions. As she said, the discrepancy involved in the airport transfer was just $1.50. Plenty of people would have let it go, and that would be fine, too. But Song-I was right to notice that her compliance had become a habit, a way of being in the world. In order to change that habit, she needed to break herself of her unconscious behaviors. She needed to start replacing some of her bad negotiation experiences with good ones.

Zappos offered Song-I her first job out of college, an exciting moment for her. But she was disappointed by the compensation offered. "I thought, this doesn't feel good. I know the job's located in Vegas and Vegas is cheap, but really? I was scared, though, and I thought, if I ask for more I'm going to be seen as needy. I'm going to be seen as demanding. I should just cut my losses and take the job. But then I challenged myself." She put a toe in the water, where she wouldn't have before. "I said, 'I'm excited to work with you guys, but the base salary is a bit low.' I was apologetic." Zappos responded with a higher base salary.

By her next job negotiation, she had dropped the need to apologize. And the negotiation after that—for the job she still has—went better still. "They had a good base salary offering," she said, but she understood there were three components at play: base salary, sign-on bonus, and stock. She dug into researching all three areas and asked detailed questions about tax exemptions before she prepared a counter-ask. "I started asking myself, Do I really care about the base salary? What is the need I'm trying to fill? And what I wanted changed." She realized that what she wanted was to make up what she'd lost from breaking her employment contract with her previous employer. She thought, too, of what need her prospective employer wanted to fulfill, and what would feel comfortable for them. They worked together to figure out a solution for all parties.

Her approach couldn't be further than the "fight to the win" mentality she grew up with. But the greatest test of Song-I's new approach to negotiation came when she was in conflict with her dad. Her family eventually moved back to South Korea, while Song-I remains in the United States. Commonly, she receives emails from her dad telling her about men he would like her to date. "At first I found it to be irritating and offensive," she said. Like me, Song-I has no interest in being set up on dates by her parents. "Then I started shifting and thinking, how do I help him see my world-view? That what he thinks is the right answer is not necessarily what I think is the right answer, and that that's okay?" They have a shared goal, she sees, which is that they both want Song-I to be happy and to live a fulfilling life. "We might have different viewpoints on what that life looks like, but we're in agreement that we both want me to be happy." Now instead of bristling and shutting down the conversation, she'll show him when she takes his advice into consideration. She's also started sharing more of her life with him, showing the ways that she is happy and fulfilled even without marriage. She's bringing him into her world a bit more and, in doing so, they are coming closer together.

When you don't ask for help

The first thing to know about Linda Schlesinger-Wagner is that she is impressive. She started the Michigan-based Internet retailer Skinnytees with a thousand-dollar loan from her friend. At the time, Linda was broke, working multiple jobs, and recently divorced. Now Skinnytees is regularly featured on *Good Morning America* and in *O* magazine and averages $4 million in sales per year. Skinnytees is heavily involved in philanthropy, and Linda is a humanitarian who has traveled the world interviewing Holocaust survivors. To look at her, you would never know just how low she has been, and how very close her life was to working out differently.

Linda grew up watching her parents run a manufacturing company, and so she was no stranger to the ups and downs of entrepreneurship. She observed everything about their tool and die company, learning all about factory and business relationships, and the ins and outs of following through on contracts. Her parents lost everything they owned when they were in their forties, and Linda watched as they picked themselves up. "They had the guts to go back in there and do it a different way," she said. Linda would follow in their footsteps in more ways than one.

As an adult, Linda was unhappily married, but, like many, stayed in her marriage to keep the family together. She opened a children's store, and shortly thereafter became a knitwear manufacturer. Her sweaters were all hand-loomed, and inspired by an antique button collection. As she was building her businesses, Linda was also her family's primary caregiver and took care of her ailing father-in-law. After her children were grown and her father-in-law had passed away, Linda told her husband that there was no longer a reason to stay together.

The divorce happened quickly, but fully separating her life from the person she'd been married to for decades was anything but easy. Though the divorce had been her idea, she found herself going back to her ex-husband, but she was so ashamed she didn't tell anyone. She was struggling with the divorce and struggling with her ex's treatment of her. As her sense of worth dipped lower and lower, she didn't want friends and family to know how bad it really was. Linda had always struggled to ask for help. Her worldview was that she should be able to handle by herself whatever life threw her way.

"My ex was emotionally and mentally abusive to me," Linda said. "I was a strong woman, and yet I thought I deserved it. The things he said to me were things that no one should say."

On one fateful day, Linda was at her former home outside Detroit, where her ex still lived. He offered her money to go buy plants and do some gardening around the house while he was out on a date. "I screamed and cried and told him how awful he was, reminding him that I was the mother of his children." Linda was inconsolable when she left the house. But she didn't want to burden anyone; she wanted to handle things on her own. She felt she *should be able to* handle things on her own. "I kept thinking that I wanted no part of this world where the person I shared my life with would treat me this way."

Linda got her hands on a bottle of Ambien. She knew a friend was out of town and drove her car near the friend's house, then ditched it and walked the rest of the way. She let herself into the empty house and laid a blanket down in a downstairs guest bathroom. She planned to slit her wrists there, but first she decided to take the Ambien. Linda was so ashamed, so low, and felt so small, that even though no one was home and no one was looking for her, she hid in an upstairs closet with a flashlight as she swallowed the pills. She was walking to the bathroom to carry out the final part of her plan when she lost consciousness. She woke up forty-eight hours later in a hospital.

That Linda survived the suicide attempt is more a factor of fortune than anything else—which is why this story is part cautionary tale. At the same time that Linda was searching for Ambien, her twenty-five-year-old daughter, halfway across the country in San Francisco, felt that something was wrong. Her mother wasn't answering her phone, which was unusual. She called Linda's cell carrier and said, "I'm worried about my mom. Can you find out where her phone is?" The carrier located the home of Linda's friend, and Linda's daughter called the police. They broke into the house, found Linda, and called an ambulance. Even then, Linda wasn't out of danger. The emergency room doctor told Linda's daughter that she was probably going to die.

But Linda did come through, and when she woke up, she remembered the emergency room nurse tending to her. The nurse told Linda, "I've been exactly where you are. Five years ago. Don't you *ever* let someone bring you down."

The aftermath of Linda's suicide attempt was bleak, as she had to stay in the psych ward before being released to a regular hospital room. Ultimately her daughter got her into The Canyon, a tony rehabilitation center in Malibu for addiction and mental health issues. It was all paid for by a friend of Linda's who knew that she would pay her back one day. "My friend picked me up and took me there," Linda said. Like it or not, Linda was being helped.

"You go down this canyon road, and there's nothing else

there—it's lush and green and hot." There were only twenty-one patients, and no one gave their last name unless they chose to.

"On my first day, the facilitators separated the women and men, and they said, 'Okay, ladies, we're going to blindfold you with a bandana. Hold the shoulders of the person in front of you. We'll lead the first person." It was slow walking for fifteen minutes, Linda said, as everyone, blindfolded, carefully stepped on what felt like a rocky path. Then the facilitators told them to hold on to a rope and to leave their blindfolds on. The facilitators explained that they were in a maze, and their task was to find the exit. "We'll make sure you don't get hurt. And if you need help, raise your hand." "In thirty seconds," Linda recounted, "they said, 'Okay, the first one has found the entrance.' Over the next minutes a bunch of others did, but I was still holding the rope. I couldn't figure out how they'd figured their way out of the maze. Then the facilitators said, 'There's two of you left. If you need help, raise your hand.' All of a sudden I understood. I said, 'Wait! I get it. If I need anything, ask for help.'" Linda had cracked the code. "I'm in the f-ing forest with people I don't know. I can't find an entrance. There wasn't an exit. The whole thing was set up to show us to ask for help. I *never* asked for help in my life. I always thought, 'I'm going to do this on my own.' It was like a giant lightbulb went off on me. I was the person who never asked for help, and who never gave up, until I tried to kill myself." That pattern, Linda understood, had held her back for much of her life.

Linda spent a month at The Canyon, then returned home to her little yellow house in Michigan to put her life back together. After her hospitalization, Linda no longer made choices that reflected her fears. "After I got out of The Canyon, I said, *I'm not going to sit in my house and have a pity party*—I put myself on JDate, on Match.com," she said, something she never would have done previously. "I met people for coffee dates." She cut off ties with her ex and started thinking of what she *wanted* to do instead of what she should do. She was set up with a friend of a friend, Paul, who had lost his wife not long before. The two had an instant connection and are now married.

Most significantly, Linda no longer delayed asking for help—from her friends and from her family. She cobbled together different jobs for a time, and then her retailer and manufacturing past gave her the inspiration for Skinnytees. She accepted a loan from a friend, something she never would have felt herself worthy of before, and started selling soft, seamless tanks that worked for all women regardless of their size.

"What happens in your personal life really spills over to your professional life," Linda said. "My personality really changed. I didn't hold back anymore. I learned to ask for help, and I ask for help all the time now." She attended the Goldman Sachs 10,000 Small Businesses program, where I met her. Linda and several others from her cohort continue to meet, years after the class has ended, to offer one another support and assistance. "Because I learned how to ask for help, that's why I think I'm eager to give help to other people," Linda said, whether it's her former classmates or the charities that she's so involved in. "We all ask each other for help. How powerful is that?"

Many people consider the negotiation process something that they have to tackle by themselves. You don't have to be the accountant who knows the financial data inside and out and the attorney who can put together comprehensive and secure contracts. We can seek professionals to help us prepare. We can talk to friends or mentors ahead of the negotiation to run through our plan and ask for critical feedback so that we have another perspective. I find that the older I get, the more comfortable I am in accepting what I don't know and asking for help. My goal is not to be the smartest person in the room. It's to be the most open to learning so that I can be wiser by the end of the conversation. I am so privileged to be surrounded by smart students, accomplished entrepreneurs, and brilliant friends and mentors. I'd be foolish not to choose access to their wisdom in order to massage my ego. When my students say, "I'm not a good negotiator because I'm so bad with numbers," my immediate response is, "Thank goodness there are so many accountants and finance professionals for you to hire!"

Always in survival mode

My student Pam was intensely competitive, sometimes to a fault, of which she was well aware. Her whole life, she had felt she *had* to be. She was an African American woman working in construction services—a white man's industry—in Detroit, a storied city with a long history of racial strife. She did not get to her position of success by tossing flowers to everyone who crossed her path—she had to roll up her sleeves and fight.

When I met Pam in 2014, she and her classmates were still recovering from the recession. When I gave her class a scenario to negotiate, she recognized it as one she'd done before. In the same way that Linda's blindfolded maze exercise was designed to give people an "aha" moment (that they needed to ask for help), this case study was designed to show people they needed to recognize that cooperation—not competition—is key.

Pam asked me if she could be excused from the exercise. She said it wouldn't be fair to the others since she knew the answer and they didn't, and she wasn't likely to get much out of it. Something told me to ask her to do it anyway, even though I usually excuse students who have done it before. What she gained from it humbled her.

"I *knew* the key. I knew we could all win if we had the right secret sauce. And still I couldn't make it happen. It went totally
wrong." She explained that she was so deeply competitive, as were
the others in her group, that the competition, guarding, and posturing overpowered collaboration. "The fact that I still couldn't
manipulate the outcome when I knew the answer was profound to
me," she said.

The intensity of Pam's competitiveness—formed over decades
of being in survival mode—made her reluctant to appear cooperative. She feared signaling vulnerability, and this fear hobbled communication and prevented Pam from creating the win-win outcome
she knew was possible.

The gift Pam got from this exercise was self-awareness—she was
able to see her scars clearly. In the future, she could use that self-
awareness to be more deliberate and proactive. Knowing her inclination to be hypercompetitive, she could be intentional; she could
create a plan that took her triggers into account. This plan might
include slowing down and taking more time at the outset of a negotiation to get to know her negotiating partner, which would soften
her more competitive inclinations. It might include waiting a few
beats before responding, checking in with herself. It might be as
simple as writing herself a note not to take any of the negotiation
personally. I don't mean to suggest that there is anything easy about
checking your strongest inclinations. There isn't. It's subtle, and it's
emotionally draining. But it can also be enormously empowering.

Haunted by an economic downturn

We are not where we are from, but our geographical reality is a
deeply embedded part of our psyche, and we need to recognize it as
such. I've taught in New Orleans, for instance, where during

hurricane season the weather report takes on huge significance. In New Orleans, it's easy to feel powerless, that your destiny is not dictated by your goals or the strength of your endeavors, because Mother Nature is there to remind you she's stronger. Through storm damage and resulting economic damage, my students in New Orleans have gotten back up again and again, but know that though they're back on their feet, any day now their doors and windows could be shuttered against a gathering hurricane. These wounds then infect the asks my students are willing to make.

"I'm a Louisiana native, so I have heavy doses of the fatalism that we're known for," said my Goldman Sachs 10,000 Small Businesses student Mary Ellen, who runs a content marketing company. "People think we like to party, but I think mostly we just figure every day could be our last, because we could be wiped off the map any minute." But she said living in Washington, D.C., for her twenties and half of her thirties helped her break out of the psychology of the region. Now that she's back in New Orleans, she'll tell her fellow New Orleanians, "Come on now, have some self-esteem! This really could work—you can do this, you can ask for that."

I've recently started teaching in Iowa and was struck by a sentiment echoed by many of my students there. There's a sense of pride and esteem, from growing up and living in "God's country." And yet there's also a lingering sense of insecurity, of imposter syndrome. It makes sense. We inhabit an economy where high tech is everything, and yet the industry has largely been centered on the coasts, while the middle of America has been skipped over, breeding uncertainty and resentment.

In the Detroit of 2014, the struggle was palpable. They were the forgotten people. As a country, we had decided that it was okay for them to fail, until it wasn't. That took a toll. Those who are still living and working in Detroit are fiercely proud, but that pride is intertwined with the vulnerabilities of their economic environment. "For many people in Detroit," said my student Pam, "there were these holes in our hearts because no matter what we tried to do, we were ridiculed. And for so many decades Detroit had been the butt of a national joke—and still is for people who don't know better." They had struggled for so long that self-doubt had infected them. Detroiters are fighters, but they had learned to expect less. Even when encouraged to request investment for their growth plans, they consistently set lower "asks." The perspectives they shared revealed a weariness, a dearth of hope.

The reasons why are clear: Say that an entrepreneur runs a small business in Detroit that supplies parts to big auto manufacturers. This entrepreneur gets an email from GM or Ford that says that because of the economy, the entrepreneur will need to cut costs by 25 percent if they're to continue to get the business. For these small Detroit-based businesses, who don't have a diverse client base, a 25 percent reduction is enormous. But they can't say no. They feel they're handcuffed, and they've felt that way for a long time. They fear the consequences of asking for more because they fear hearing no. They don't try to find a solution that may work for both parties. They think, *How can I possibly do well negotiating with someone who has so much leverage?* Although certainly there are other company towns, and big corporations often employ bullying tactics with those they work with, it's different in Detroit. Chicago and Pittsburgh had troubles, too, and after Boeing cut jobs in Seattle in the 1970s, someone erected a soon-to-be famous billboard that read: *Will the last person leaving Seattle—Turn out the lights*. But Chicago, Pittsburgh, and Seattle diversified—they were not solely dependent on the industries that put them on the map. These cities also didn't suffer as much from the deeply ingrained racial issues that plagued Detroit. These cities didn't stay beaten down and poor for decades or suffer from a consistent lack of leadership. These cities were wounded but not scarred like Detroit. If a human being becomes depressed from being tired and stressed for a long period of time, it only makes sense that the same conditions would apply for a region that's had bad news for years.

To really understand the impact of these economic scars, it's illuminating to look at someone from Detroit who *doesn't* have them, and the ways the world looks different. Andrew Chmielewski grew up in a suburb of Detroit and was still in school during the worst of the economic downturn. He was passionate about business, though, and noticed a great opportunity when his dad, Dave—a retired Detroit firefighter—started getting more requests for his homemade toffee than he could handle. Dave was a great cook and often baked for his old engine house, but the demand for the toffee was unlike anything he'd encountered before. Andrew left school to grow the toffee into a business, and ten years later, Dave's Sweet Tooth Toffee is in five thousand stores.

"I'm thirty," Andrew said, "so ten years ago, I wasn't involved in the economy in any meaningful way. I didn't have a mortgage or a business." Having grown up amid the downtimes, he came of age aware but not scarred. He was pleasantly surprised that it wasn't difficult to convince people to give him money. He saw his Detroit roots not as a weight but as a plus: He didn't have to compete with all of the stylish indie brands coming out of Brooklyn or San Francisco, where Dave's Sweet Tooth might have gotten lost. He could experiment with flavors in a home kitchen, try and fail different recipes, and just generally be creative, all without being under anyone's thumb.

His confidence in his product and in the market built on itself. At thirty, he's comfortable walking away from big corporate accounts if they won't come to a reasonable agreement, and he pointed out, "You can't lose what you don't have, right?" He knows, of course, that the potential with those accounts is massive. But that's just the point—Andrew sees potential everywhere.

Few of us get through life unscarred, of course, and Andrew will surely have his share of trials. The key, though, is to be aware of how those trials are shaping your outlook and your decisions. The key is to let them inform you but not hurt you.

My fear of failure, I learned, was my scar, and it could be debilitating. My fear of calling it quits on my company led me to make some terrible financial decisions and to stay in a job that didn't make me happy. I was letting it define me.

But there's another side of my scar, too. Even as I limped on with the company, I enrolled in business school at Wharton. I loved it, and I thrived, earning accolades from my peers and professors. During my second semester of business school I was in a horrible car accident when another car hit me going fifty miles per hour. I broke my ribs and all of my metatarsals, but when I was released from the emergency room I still stayed up to study cost accounting all night because I was terrified of flunking out. I was in a cast for four months, and somehow through my recovery, I kept up my grades. I would not skip classes, I would not fail at school. My fear of failure, I learned, could be motivating.

I ended up giving the graduation address for my class at Wharton. I remember standing pridefully before my family in the audience, and before my classmates and professors, and thinking that I had done it, that I had earned this. I could let the scars of my business define me, or I could let this moment define me. I chose the latter and have never looked back.

I'm much more mindful about my scars now. I catch myself when I'm up against a decision and my fear of failure rears its head. I can tell when my judgment is affected by imposter syndrome, or when the words in my head are my parents', not mine. I know this is a struggle for me, and that likely it always will be. But now I can look at it more objectively. I can tell if I'm stewing in the midst of old baggage, which doesn't serve me, or looking to a future with the lessons of my past relegated to their rightful place on the sidelines. And I feel fortunate to have caught myself out. The real danger is when you don't even realize that your scars are there at all.

CHAPTER 4

getting the how *wrong*

N elson Mandela may well have been the best negotiator of
the twentieth century. What he wanted—equal citizenship
for blacks, an end to South African apartheid—was nothing
short of monumental. As he served a life sentence in prison, he had
every right and reason to scream his demands. But what made Mandela so brilliant, and ultimately so effective, was his ability to separate his powerful feelings and to empathize with his jailers, as well
as with all of those who would love nothing more than to see apartheid thrive. He was a pragmatist. He patiently considered what approach would resonate not only with the South African government
but also with the African National Congress. From prison, he was
able to bring these two sides together by gently leading from behind,
understanding what each side needed to hear and how each needed
to approach talking to the other. He had grown up watching his father, a tribal chief, build consensus, and noted how the chief "stays
behind the flock, letting the most nimble go ahead, whereupon the
others follow, not realizing they are being led from behind."

Abraham Lincoln used a similar patient, empathetic approach, once claiming: "When I get ready to talk to people, I spend two thirds of the time thinking what they want to hear and one third thinking about what I want to say."

The average person may not be as skilled at communication as Mandela or Lincoln, but we do carefully calculate how to present information to a particular audience all the time, starting from when we were kids and knew to wait until Mom and Dad were in a good mood to ask if we could have dessert. Despite this, when an exchange is framed as a negotiation, we often forget the soft skills—that we are dealing, first and foremost, with another human being.

Whenever you negotiate—whether it's about changing risky be-havior, closing a complex business deal, or deciding who is going to take the garbage out—you need to know two things: what you're going to ask for, and how. Most people spend considerable time and energy worrying about what to ask for, whether their ask is justi-fied, and whether they're asking for too much or too little. But they spend little if any time thinking about how to frame their argu-ment. They don't stop to consider, "How will my counterpart receive the information if I ask this way? What about if I ask it another way?"

For years, my friend Clay worked in diplomatic protocol. He was the guy prepping politicians and government officials on what they needed to know before multicultural events. He would brief them on where the country flags should be placed, how—or whether!—to shake someone's hand, and even why the color of their clothing mattered. Each year, I bring him in to speak to my negotiation classes, not because they need to know the finer points of gift giving in a business meeting with bilateral partners, but because they do need to understand how much the details matter and how much they can signal.

This chapter is about communication. When the *how* of our communication gets rushed, when you don't put the thought into it that's required, it creates a lot of unnecessary problems and unfavorable results. In this chapter, I look at the ways we get the *how* of the ask so wrong, and why.

You can't rush a good deal

Most of us follow rules that we feel are "truisms"—which, by definition, are statements so obvious they aren't even worth mentioning. We avoid dairy if we have a cold, thinking that it increases mucus production (it doesn't). We drop our sandwich on the floor but then pick it up quickly, thinking, "five-second rule"—when, in actuality, time has nothing to do with bacteria's ability to infect our food. And of course, everybody knows that it's always better to be efficient than not. Wrong again.

Let's get right to the point, shall we? Americans are nothing if not efficient. Why just drive when you can drive, eat, and make a work call at the same time? Why wait in a line at the grocery store when you can order delivery from Instacart? People are able to accomplish more in a day than ever before, and as to-do lists grow, social niceties are seen as a waste of precious time. "I should be able to close this deal and go home in a day or so" is a common refrain from American businesspeople. They imagine flying to Tokyo, meeting their client in person for the first time, signing the deal, then flying home the next day. They'll be able to order groceries on the plane, and maybe even get caught up on email.

Regardless of whether that's the way business should be done (and I would argue it isn't), quick transactions aren't realistic and rarely make for the most ideal outcomes. Particularly in cultures that put an emphasis on relationships—like those in Asia, Latin America, and the Middle East—people want to know who they're doing business with. Dinners, drinks, and conversation all take place before broaching business. Relationships mean more than the transaction. It's a courting process, and even in more task-oriented cultures like Germany and the United States, relationships matter. Robert Iger, who was the CEO of Disney, met in person with George Lucas over a period of *two years* when negotiating the purchase of Lucasfilm, and he told the *New York Times* of the deal with the *Star Wars* visionary, "There was a lot of trust there." Simply put, negotiation requires patience. People are still people and want to see and be seen by whoever they're negotiating with.

Glen Cutrona has worked in real estate development in New York for decades. He says many of the people he deals with for permitting at government agencies are "disgruntled, not happy about what they do." His job, he's come to see, "is to get them to feel comfortable enough to drop their guard . . . I can't walk into scenarios thinking 'I must get this done.' Everything you do is a negotiation. Everybody wants something faster than you can deliver it. But it takes time, and I've learned to be involved with people. I have to consider the fact that I'm going to be involved with these people in five years."

Perhaps the most stereotypically efficient environment is that of a financial trading floor, which is where Anthony Chiarito got his start. He went straight from high school to a job at the Chicago Mercantile Exchange. "Not a place," he said, "where you show emotion. It was a very testosterone-filled environment." He spent a decade there before moving on to the insurance field, and he now runs his own insurance agency. He felt that some of what he learned at the exchange, such as where to take risks, has helped, but some elements of the culture have hindered him. "I get too quickly to the point," he said, "and don't let my personality come out." Though a naturally friendly and outgoing guy, Anthony always thought he should shut that side of himself off in negotiation. "I could build a rapport, I just didn't allow myself to. If I'm pursuing something I'm more reserved. I thought that was the way to be, to keep it to business."

When Anthony realized his formal approach wasn't serving him well, he adjusted. He recently opened up a second location for his insurance business, which required him to find an office space. "Originally the price was right but the square footage wasn't," he said of a place he liked. "What I wanted to do was hurry up, get it wrapped up, and move on to the next thing." But he slowed down. He built a rapport with the building owners. He brought his wife to tour the space. "They got to know me, to see that I was responsible," he said. "So they allowed me to go in at a month-to-month, and for the rent to be at a lower square footage unit."

If you *don't* take the time to build connection but go straight into the bargaining, then if you reach an impasse regarding your numbers, there's nothing else to talk about. There's no context, no building of affiliation. Organizations that write grants for government jobs consistently say that the hardest ones to write are those based only on pricing. If you're not offering to do the job for the least amount, you're out. There are no other data points, no other information exchange. In contrast, consider what happens in a hot housing market: Buyers write personal notes to the sellers, often including a photo of themselves or their family. Under the rules of game theory, the highest bidder would win, end of story. That still *does* happen, and yet when offers are close, it makes a difference to remind people they're doing business with a human being, not a number.

When you build rapport, when you take time to have conversations and learn about one another, it does make the process longer. It might even increase the duration by an entire sales cycle. But now your counterpart has other pieces of information that he can use to make a decision or further build the relationship. The exchange has become more than just a transaction. We'll dig deeper into building relationships in Part II.

"Nice guys finish last"

In the 1975 book *Anatomy of a Merger*, superlawyer James C. Freund wrote, "Everyone has his [or her] own negotiating style, and the worst thing you can do is to adopt a negotiating technique that does not feel comfortable [because] credibility, based on an evident sincerity, is the most important single asset of a good negotiator." Nearly fifty years later, legions of young negotiators still struggle to take this advice to heart.

Jennifer, the graphic designer I introduced in Chapter 1, was one of these negotiators. After years of work and friendship with her business partners, Jennifer decided to leave the company she'd cofounded. The buyout process made her extremely nervous; not only was she a pleaser, but conversations about money at her company had been very morally loaded.

As a result, Jennifer turned to her husband for help settling her buyout. He was an attorney and had long rolled his eyes when Jennifer expressed her reluctance to talk money with her partners. His culture was the polar opposite: Any reference to feelings or moralizing about negotiation was scoffed at. This was business, not personal.

Jennifer's husband drafted all of the correspondence she wrote to her partners about the buyout. Once they got a number from a third-party appraiser, Jennifer's husband ghostwrote an email that listed all the reasons they should agree to the number and do so immediately. It was formal and filled with legalese meant to get the deal agreed to quickly. Jennifer added a line of her own at the end of it, indicating her great affection for her partners, and sent it.

Jennifer's partners, though they agreed to the number, were upset with her. They felt her approach was overly formal and confrontational. They felt she hadn't honored the close and personal nature of their decadelong relationship. Only much later, when she had a heart-to-heart with one of her former partners, Carrie, did she learn the extent of their hurt.

"I don't know that you realized what it was like to get that email," Carrie said. "We'd been having a really tough year financially, which I thought you understood, and here we were hit with this demanding, honestly kind of mean, email. And then the way you ended it with all this affection was just weird. It was like, *Does she really not have a clue how she came across here?*" What's particularly ironic about this story is that Jennifer was emotionally intelligent—it was one of her strongest traits. But she was so panicked by negotiation and so sure that her emotional intelligence would only serve to harm her that she shut off what could have been her greatest asset. She explained all of this to Carrie, Carrie owned up to her own mistakes in the process, and the two have resumed a close friendship. Still, it was a messy process that was unnecessary, and Jennifer is still not on speaking terms with one of her other partners.

Jennifer and I debriefed the experience together because though she knew where she'd messed up, she wanted to know how she could have done it differently. The answer was all in the communication, all in the how. "You might have thought through how your partners would receive your ask, knowing that they put a moral judgment on it," I said. "Didn't they once tell you that when you lead conversations by talking about money, it makes them distrust you?"

Jennifer reddened. "They're wrong to do that. They shouldn't— it's business." She was echoing the logic of her lawyer husband and his culture.

"But they do," I reminded her, pointing out the importance of being pragmatic. We talked through how she might have couched her ask in a way that would speak to her partners. They valued relationship. She could have started there. They adored their brand. She could have gone there next. Instead of leading with formality and numbers, she could have simply met them where they were, and made the ask make sense to them in language they could relate to.

"Gender doesn't matter" (but emotional intelligence does)

Although this section also relates to men, it's undeniable that the bias here swings more one way than the other. You're right. Like her or not, never was gender bias more evident than with the presidential candidacy of Hillary Clinton. Everything she said, did, and wore was filtered through the lens of her sex. Gender stereotypes are real. Study after study shows that the achievements of women are viewed more critically than the same achievements of men.

When women make an ask, they often face consequences that men wouldn't. Women who are not afraid to initiate negotiations and who will ask for more may be seen as demanding and aggressive. They are seen as less likable and pushy, whereas their male counterparts are viewed as goal-oriented and skilled negotiators for doing the same things.

Female business owners, particularly in male-dominated industries, are highly cognizant of this dilemma and double standard. Likability is important, and they can't afford to be seen as pushy, greedy, or aggressive. (They likely aren't any of these things, but in negotiation, perception is reality.) So what to do?

For starters, women don't have to ask for less. What they do have to do is focus on making the ask appeal to their counterpart. Their preparation requires them not only to understand their own interests, set high goals, and identify information that supports those goals, but to take into consideration their counterpart's perspective and interests. Emotional intelligence is everything. If you have your pulse on the emotions, reactions, and receptivity of your counterpart, you can navigate the conversation with precision. This isn't true just for women—it's true for everyone, and in every negotiation.

Even as they make the ask, women think we can frame it less as an extra battle we need to fight and more as a celebration of our skill. When my former student Eszter, a fantastic businesswoman, successfully negotiated for a table at a full restaurant, the men she was with teased her that she used the fact that she's a young woman to get her way. This irked her, because she knew she used her intelligence and her savvy, and she felt they were shortchanging her skill. She hadn't just batted her eyelashes and magically secured a table—she had made a point of connecting with the maître d', casting herself as his partner to come up with creative solutions. When she asked my take on it, I told her that her femininity was wrapped up in her keen emotional intelligence, so yes, she had used it, and—by the way—it was effective. Instead of seeing it as demeaning, she could see it as a compliment. She had used her warmth and her compassion as sources of power. It's the same sentiment Ava DuVernay, who directed the Oscar-nominated film *Selma* as well as the female-strong *A Wrinkle in Time*, expressed when she told the *New*

York Times, "When you say 'feminizing,' people think of softness in certain places, but I think of strength in other places." That's what Eszter had exhibited.

In my work in the sports industry, my femininity is always there as subtext. I could go into a meeting as the only woman and think, "Oh, you're expecting Jane? Well, too bad, guys, I'm Tarzan!" Plenty of women use that strategy. But that wouldn't be being true to who I am. I might play up or play down certain characteristics based on my audience, but I'm always authentically myself. I will compliment certain people because I'm paying attention and I can tell that it will help set the tone I want. That's not kissing up—it's having emotional intelligence. I wouldn't give a compliment I couldn't stand behind, or ask a question I didn't genuinely want to know the answer to.

When my female students explain, "I'm working in a male-dominated industry and never know how to handle it. I'm so worried about appearing like I'm flirting, or being too nice," I tell them never to apologize for being a woman. Use all of your weapons, including the emotional intelligence that many women are so good at. Giving someone a compliment is fair game, so long as you mean it. Wearing a low-cut blouse or a short skirt to attract attention is not.

Importantly, using emotional intelligence does not mean rolling over, and the minute I feel disrespected I will call it out. My boundaries are clear and I set a high standard for how I expect to be treated—not as a woman but as a human being. I no longer have trouble speaking up for myself, and I always tell women to do so. But I'm also not going to play the angry woman because I feel like men have marginalized me my whole life. That won't get me anywhere either. It may not be fair that we constantly have to think about these nuances, but it's the way it is . . . for now.

Business *is* personal

My student Pam, the owner of the construction services company in Detroit, learned this lesson—as she's learned most—the hard way. "I didn't understand the necessity of relationship," Pam said, then elaborated that she meant, "people who want the best for you, who aren't related to you, but there's something in you they want to engage with long-term. People willing to spend their social capital on you. I differentiated 'this is business' and 'this is personal.'" In 2012, Pam lost an order that would have changed her life. It took her two years to realize why she had lost it, given that she had been advised by the purchaser that she had the best price and the best technical offer. "The other company received the order on the strength of their relationship," Pam said simply.

"Before I lost the order, I knew intellectually that people do business with people they know. But I truly believed that if I worked hard, and did great work, I would win." It took some time for Pam to get past the loss. "After I lost the order, I was hurt and angry, but I really *got it*. I had underestimated the strength of comfort and camaraderie or relationships in business. In the past, I would have viewed the loss as racist and sexist. But I realized that it was less intentional than that. White men still control contracts. Because their primary relationships are with other white men, they're purchasing from a pool of business owned and operated by white men. Typically, they're not intentional about meeting other people. They don't necessarily know African American women and Latina women. And if they don't know us, then we're not in the pool, and we don't have access to relationships or the opportunities. I had to change that."

Once she understood this, Pam changed her approach. Her new business plan? "Y'all gonna know me." Pam has spent the last four years stepping out of everything that's comfortable to her. She's on panels, she does keynotes, she gets her name out every chance she can. Putting herself out there was the missing link. She and her business are now known entities. "It has worked remarkably well," she said. "But it was the hardest and most important lesson that I've learned."

The problem of overconfidence

When you are overconfident, you mess up the *how*. And when I say *overconfident*, don't immediately exclude yourself because you're a modest sort of person. Overconfidence is an easy trap to fall into. Many people spend years working on their confidence and are right to do so, as it's critical for their negotiation. I'm all for confidence. (See Chapter 1!) But it's a very slippery slope before it turns into overconfidence, and overconfidence can affect the most humble of us. When it does, it keeps us from preparing to the extent we should.

Anthony Chiarito's experience at the Chicago Mercantile Exchange, as well as in business afterward, made him feel pretty confident about his negotiation ability. Negotiation was not something that scared him when he arrived in his cohort's negotiation class for Goldman Sachs's 10,000 Small Businesses. "I wasn't arrogant coming into the class," he said, "but I was really confident."

Overconfident, as it turned out.

In a class exercise, Anthony's role was to sell a rare piece of jewelry. The amount that he'd charged for jewelry from this designer, and this particular line, had gone up consistently year over year. He also had made one special-occasion sale, but it was an off-market deal between him and a friend, and the price point they'd agreed on was significantly lower than his public sales.

When Anthony planned his negotiation strategy, he used that off-market sale as a data point, which brought his year-over-year growth curve down. As a result, he didn't set his goal high enough. This first mistake was a problem of preparation, because in reality that data point did not need to be factored in—it was an outlier.

Second, he shared the information about the off-market sale freely, which hurt the case about the rate of rising value for the jewelry.

I'm generally a supporter of sharing information. People tend to hold information too close, which cuts off creative thinking and hinders openly exploring areas of mutual gain. (This is the subject of Chapter 8!) But before going into a negotiation, you have to think about whether each piece of information at your disposal works to your advantage if you share it or puts you at a disadvantage. Anthony *should* share information about his past public sales and how the value of the jewelry had consistently and dramatically gone up (as rare objects often do). This information was freely available anyway, and by sharing it, Anthony would establish the tone of the conversation as one of openness and explain why he was justified in his ask. The information about the off-market sale, in contrast, didn't help Anthony. It shouldn't have hurt him, since there were good reasons why that amount was lower, but he hadn't really thought that part through.

If Anthony had not been overconfident, he would have prepared more. And if he had prepared more, he would have known not to share the information about the off-market sale but to be ready—if asked—to provide that information along with an explanation of why that sale was lower in order to diminish the information's influence.

He was surprised when he and his partner finished negotiating before most of the others. "I was in a rush to get at it. I was one of the first people done. That was eye-opening to me."

He was even more surprised when I displayed the results of the first negotiation. (Remember, everybody sees everybody else's results on a screen, and then we debrief them.) Not only was Anthony's deal one of the first ones completed, but he came out near the bottom. "In real-life negotiations, you don't have the chance to figure out what the other side was willing to pay," Anthony said. "You get a deal and think you did a great job.

"It was an awakening to me," he said, "that my confidence was not well placed. I made my notes, I made my plan. The failure was right there in the planning. I didn't understand what my position should have been, but I thought I knew it. I should have given more thought to it. I lost the negotiation before I opened my mouth. That exercise showed me that there was a better process. That I needed to slow down."

Beware of overconfidence, because it can trap you into shorting your preparation. There is someone out there who is concerned they're not prepared enough, and they're preparing more than you. They are crossing every *t* and dotting every *i*, and unless you have, too, and have a solid explanation for your ask that you believe in, they will get a better deal.

I want my students to be confident, but I want them to come to their confidence organically rather than coming in and saying, "I know this stuff cold" without an appropriate level of preparation.

Another by-product of overconfidence is that the overconfident negotiator will try to sell something for more than they can justify. Remember from Chapter 1 that you tell a story that's favorable to you, but that's based in data. That story can't be a fairy tale. I've watched numerous businesses that are acquisition targets seek unrealistic sales goals. They never get what they want and sacrifice their credibility in the process.

I see similar dynamics in almost every single class I teach. In just one recent example, when a student named Jane was selling a tonic, she set her price at $4 an ounce when the data could really only support a sale of $2.

When I asked her why she did this, she said, "The buyer represented a pharmaceutical company."

That didn't clear it up for me, so I asked her to explain.

"I work in pharma," she said. "They have tons of money."

I hear similar and very dangerous assumptions like this one all the time, from every gender and age of student. It will come as no surprise that Jane's strategy didn't work. In fact, when her price was so far above what the buyer could (or expected to) pay, she almost got left out of the deal completely. Although she ultimately sold her tonic for $1.50 an ounce, she had hurt her credibility by anchoring so high.

The problem was that Jane hadn't thought through the *how* of the ask. She knew what she wanted but couldn't verbalize why in a way that made sense. If the buyer asked, "How did you arrive at $4?" Jane would have nothing to say other than, "Because I think you can afford it," which would not have gone over well. You don't offend people by making rational, justifiable asks, but you do offend them when the ask doesn't make sense.

Again, I have a similar conversation in almost every class. The specifics of the exercise may be different, the experience of the student may be different, but what's always consistent is that when I push them to explain why they came up with the price they asked for, their answer is a variation of "Because I thought I could get it." They've compromised the *how*.

Moving beyond our traps

The chapters in this book have thus far only covered half of the issue: what gets in our way. There's still much work to be done though. What do you know about your negotiation partner? How will you learn more? How can you see your differences as a problem to be solved rather than a battle to win? How can you claim and maintain leverage? You can ask these questions, and others that make up Part II, once you have a handle on who you are and where you're coming from—and then and only then can you look across the table.

In the way that I view negotiation, coming to an agreement with your counterpart is an important step, but it's not the end of the exchange. Because once you've done the work together to come to a mutual solution, you have—first of all—a doorway to other mutual solutions in the future. You have a relationship, shared equity, and a shared vision. Every conversation thereafter is easier, because there is trust. From this vantage, you can then say, "Let's take a step back. Can we do even better than this deal?" And from there, you get beyond just yes.

part II

what gets us beyond yes

I HAVE DISCOVERED IN
LIFE THAT THERE ARE
WAYS OF GETTING
ALMOST ANYWHERE YOU
WANT TO GO, IF YOU
REALLY WANT TO GO.
—LANGSTON HUGHES

CHAPTER 5

the power of an open mind

We all pay lip service to the notion that understanding both sides of an issue is important, as is keeping an open mind. Many of us grew up with the moralizing of Atticus Finch in our heads: "You never really understand a person until you consider things from his point of view." And yet we don't do it—not really. In a recent study, 202 Americans were asked their views on same-sex marriage, then given a choice: Read several statements supporting that position, answer some questions about it, and make $7. Or they could read several statements supporting the opposing view, answer some questions about it, and make $10. No one was asking them to *change* their view in any way, the time requirement was the same, and yet 64 percent of people who supported same-sex marriage chose to take less money so as not to have to read the opposing view, and 61 percent of same-sex marriage opponents felt the same way. It seems we just don't want to hear the other side of the story.

Having an open mind means, first and foremost, being curious. You have to ask questions—not just of your counterpart but of yourself. It requires being authentic, of really and truly wanting to know more. It requires asking the "why" questions and being disciplined and patient enough to learn the answers. It doesn't matter if that question is "Why is my dad so controlling?" or "Why does she want to buy this particular car?" It requires being sensitive to your biases, acknowledging that of course you have them. It requires skills in the art of conversation and a willingness to employ them, even if you're an introvert who really dreads these kinds of interactions. So although knowing that you should bring an open mind into a negotiation is one thing, actually doing so is far more difficult.

An introspective mind is an open mind

Before you can engage with your counterpart in a negotiation, you first have to be introspective, and that involves asking more questions. What do you *really* want? What is your *interest*? Don't just assume that you know.

Critical to every negotiation is the issue of interest and positions, and the difference between them. It's a pretty nuanced topic, but here's how I think of it: When you use Google Maps (or any other navigation app), you first input your desired destination and then the point from which you're starting out. Google Maps in turn gives you a variety of routes based on whether you're driving, taking public transportation, or walking. All these routes or modes of transport get you to your destination. In negotiation, your interest is your destination (desired outcome) and all the different routes you could possibly take to get to your destination are your positions.

Put another way, your interest is the reason you're engaged in a negotiation in the first place and what motivates you to come to the table. Your interest is your underlying need, want, fear, or desire, and it doesn't have to be mutually exclusive from that of your counterpart. Your positions are all the possible options you have to achieve your interest. Positions are often confused with interest because they're easier to grasp and communicate. For instance, let's say that you're negotiating a new contract with a long-standing, highly valued client. The cost of doing business has increased over the years, and so you would love to somehow get a larger contract. Going into the meeting with your client, you may think that your interest in the negotiation is to get more money for that new contract. But rarely is money what brought you to the bargaining table. You want to secure a larger contract, certainly, but what you *really* want and *need* is to maintain the relationship with the client. This is a major account and one you can't afford to lose. It's steady work, they pay on time, and they offer a sense of security in your income projections. Therefore, more funding is not what matters most—it's the relationship and, once you spend the time preparing, you're well aware of that.

If you drill deep to understand your interest prior to the conversation, thinking carefully about what's bringing you to the negotiation in the first place, you know that although you would like to get paid more for your work, there are many ways to get you to what you really want—that long-standing, stable relationship with a great client. In your preparation, you'd think about various scenarios that would meet your interest. Perhaps you could suggest that the client sign a multiyear contract, which would give you more stability, or better payment terms, which would give you a healthier cash flow. These options fulfill your interest, meet your immediate funding needs, and provide you with a variety of possibilities to present to the client that could work for them as well.

Alternatively, let's say that you only scratched the surface in your thinking and approached the meeting focused on obtaining a larger contract, with a specific amount in mind. When you sit down together, you ask for more money for the work. The client says no. Where do you go from there? You have not considered any alternatives to offer them when they don't concur with a larger contract. They tell you that they haven't budgeted for it. Their *no* sticks because you can't move on to another potential solution that could be mutually acceptable. Your thinking is limited, and the negotiation comes to a dead stop.

Song-I went through this process in her job negotiation that I wrote about in Chapter 3. Initially she thought she would just ask for a higher salary, but she stopped herself to question her true desires and see the 360 view. There were three factors in play—salary, sign-on bonus, and benefits. Which mattered most to her, and why? Only after reflecting more deeply on her needs and wants was she able to recognize her true interest: She wanted to make up what she lost by leaving her previous company before her contract was up. That gave her a lot of room to negotiate—she could get to this interest in numerous ways, and work with her new would-be employer to do it.

Let's consider a more personal example, one that most couples with children encounter at some point. Two parents are negotiating who will pick their daughter up from camp at rush hour. The mom thinks, *Dammit, it's his turn, he has to do it. I don't have enough time, I'm doing everything around here, I've got a million things to do that don't involve sitting in traffic.* Let's imagine the dad's thought process is similar. If they go into their negotiation without questioning and understanding their own underlying interest fully, chances are excellent they'll battle.

The mom's position is that she wants to be free of driving duty that day. But her interest is more nuanced. What she really wants is to feel less tired and overwhelmed. She wants to feel more supported by her husband. The dad has a big deadline at the end of the day that's going to be difficult to complete if he has to leave early. His position is that he wants to be free of driving duty that day, but his interest is that he wants enough time to get his work done. If the mom and dad aren't thinking through their interests, they can't see the many positions actually available to them. The mom could agree to pick up their daughter since her husband has a deadline but, in order to honor her feelings of being overwhelmed, ask that he take something else off her plate, or perhaps that he offer to do pickup every other day that week. The dad might think of a friend he could call who also has a child at that camp, and they could sort out a carpool. But the parents can't get to that place without uncovering their true interest.

When you're clear about what's truly driving you, you can turn your curiosity toward the person you're negotiating with. What are their interests? You may not know—and you'll want to carefully make some assumptions. You'll pressure-test these assumptions in conversation, but first you need to make some educated guesses.

Gather information. Be a detective. You want to discover everything you possibly can about your counterpart. Revenue at my student Mary Ellen Slayter's marketing company is up 40 percent in the last couple of years, and she credits the rise in part to the fact that she now takes much more time gathering information about her counterpart's possible interests. She explained that although there are many details about a meeting she can't control, "I can control what I know about the people I'm meeting with and what they need," she said. "That doesn't require me to be smart or have some exotic skill, that literally just requires me to go read the LinkedIn profiles of people before I talk to them, try to ask if there's a deck they want me to review before we meet, to Google to see whatever initiatives they've had. That's not some secret skill. That just takes time."

But here's where curiosity about your counterpart gets particularly tricky, because as you prepare, and as you negotiate, you have to watch out for bias. Bias can take many forms and can lead you to faulty thinking that hurts your negotiation. And lest you think you're free of bias, let me assure you that you're not.

Confronting your biases

We often think that people with whom we interact, manage, befriend, hire, and do business with think similarly to us. As we prepare to negotiate, we consider information that *we* feel is important, and presume that it will be important to our counterpart. To negotiate effectively, though, you need to question any biases you may have. This means that you can't take the starting point for granted.

Consider the use of the word *fair*. I constantly have students tell me that they just wanted to be fair, or that so-and-so wasn't playing fair. But *fair* means something different to everyone. It can be very hard to get on the same page as others because we make assumptions based on our own values, experiences, and—importantly—our culture. Americans may think it's only fair to get complimentary tap water when dining out, but in many European countries that's an unreasonable presumption. In some families it's expected that whoever is hosting a dinner will do all of the dishes afterward, whereas in others such a scenario would seem wrong. Our values are very personal to each of us and are derived from a variety of factors (age, race, gender, education, socioeconomic status). This is why the word *fair* can be fraught. Fair to who? Fair by what standards? If your values are different, then the way you evaluate fairness must be different. If you want to appeal to someone's sense of fairness, it's important to put yourself in their shoes to really understand what *they* would consider fair—it's all about perspective.

In an exercise my classes do, each group has access to a lifesaving dialysis machine but must choose who from a select list of candidates will receive it. Should it go to the mother charged with taking care of a large family? To the doctor whose work saves lives? To the employer whose role providing jobs in the community is critical? Or to a child who has so much life left to live? This is almost always a heated negotiation, and was especially so for one of my recent classes. The discussion and outrage over what was fair and what wasn't was so intense that it took up the better part of two classes. The problem was, there were forty-eight students and thus forty-eight different perspectives on what the word *fair* meant. The groups that were the most successful had decided on a metric— criteria for making the choice. How were they evaluating who they chose? The value the person would have on society? How they would provide for the people they took care of? Age? When they could establish these norms, they could then apply them to every one of the people being considered for the machine. It was still hard to come up with a metric everyone could agree on, but it was the only way to get even close to a solution.

I've no intention of boycotting the word *fair* but encourage using it wisely by asking a question: "What does fair mean to you?" Words matter in a negotiation. You have to be discerning and methodical. The word *fair* is neither.

"It's not fair that she got X and I didn't," said every little brother or sister *ever*. But what does that mean, really? My sister often bemoaned the fact that since I was the youngest, I was spoiled, that it wasn't "fair" when my parents did (fill in the blank). In my view, she'd had it much easier, because she only had my mom and dad to parent her, whereas I had my parents, my sister, and my older brother. I effectively had four parents, and *that* felt unfair. But how was she supposed to understand my reasoning? Her experience was hers and mine was mine. If all we did was argue about what was fair, we'd get nowhere.

We *all* have false preconceptions like these. A false bias can be based on racial stereotypes, a theme played with in both the films *BlacKkKlansman* and *Sorry to Bother You*, wherein an African American character adopts a "white" telephone voice. The words are just words, but the perception of the person on the other end of the line is vastly different. A false bias is assuming a pilot is a "he," or that a nurse is a "she." We base our ideas on artificial information, and then we're surprised when we find our assumptions to be wrong. I teach this stuff, and still I'm guilty of it! Once just recently I was checking out an investment property and had arranged to meet the owner there. This guy showed up, looking unshowered and disheveled, wearing raggedy clothes and with his hair looking like Albert Einstein's. I was thinking I should offer him some money, but then he reached out his hand to shake mine. "Hi, I'm Jack," he said, and explained that he was the building owner. I thought, *Wait, what? You own this building?* I recovered my powers of speech but vowed to check myself more closely for bias.

Jennifer Eberhardt has spent years studying bias, won a Mac-Arthur Genius Grant for her work, and published a brilliant book on the subject. She spent the first few years of her life living in an African American neighborhood, and she noticed when her family moved to a white neighborhood that the school was nicer, that the resources were better. She also noticed that all of her new white friends looked the same. So much so, in fact, that she had a hard time telling them apart. So began a lifelong fascination with the way that biases affect us and what we can do about it. As she learned, her childhood reaction was normal. "That cringeworthy expression 'They all look alike' has long been considered the province of the bigot," she wrote. "But it is actually a function of biology and exposure. Our brains are better at processing faces that evoke a sense of familiarity."

Eberhardt has studied the ways that bias is triggered by stress, an issue she looked at closely with police departments with whom she's worked. Even if officers are aware of their biases, she said, biases can still be triggered in situations where the officer is stressed, is threatened, or has to make decisions fast. "We cannot possibly take in all of the stimuli with which we are constantly bombarded. Based on our goals and our expectations, we make choices—often unconsciously—about what we attend to and what we do not." One way to gird against bias, then, is to slow everything down to the extent you can. She told NPR of her work with the Oakland, California, police department. "They decided to change their foot pursuit policies. And so instead of chasing someone, you know, they were told to step back and set up a perimeter and call for backup."

So what does this look like in the far less consequential area of a business negotiation? Researchers distinguish between two types of thinking: System 1 thinking, which is quick and grounded in intuition; and System 2 thinking, which is slower and more conscious. (Daniel Kahnemann's *Thinking, Fast and Slow* is great for reading more on the subject.) The key with stripping bias out of your negotiation—particularly those that are more consequential than whether your child gets a second cookie—is to make sure you're working from System 2. Be mindful, and slow it way down. Think about time-share pitches—there's a reason the salespeople insist they get an answer that very day in order to make the deal; they know that it puts the buyer in their System 1 mind. Finally, Eberhardt cautions to be aware that bias is a state, not a trait. Be on the lookout for the state you're in.

If you're trying to imagine your counterpart's interest before a difficult conversation or negotiation, you might seek advice and counsel from others so that you can anticipate reactions that you may not have considered. But if you just ask those who agree with you, you're vulnerable to *confirmation bias*. You're at risk for becoming more cemented in your ideas and are thrown when, during the negotiation, a perspective is raised that you hadn't thought of before. You have to intentionally seek opinions from people who will challenge your thinking. Get other points of view and fight any inclination not to be open to them. Kai Ryssdal, the host of *Marketplace* on NPR, asked a group of adoring progressives how many of them listened to conservative Rush Limbaugh's show or watched Fox News occasionally. No one raised a hand, and he chastised the crowd, saying that it was their responsibility to listen to and understand the other side, not just to talk to others who felt just as they did. This is obviously uncomfortable to do but imperative for any negotiation.

Some of my consulting projects involve talking to organizations about how to create more diverse and inclusive organizations to retain top talent, promote greater engagement, drive innovation, and improve overall business outcomes. The connection between this work and negotiation may not be obvious, but I talk about the same characteristics and encourage people to use the same skills. Foremost among them is countering confirmation bias. You cannot have an effective organization if you have only one type of person making decisions.

The need to diversify does not come from an altruistic or politically correct place—though those are nice benefits. It comes from a place of smart strategy, from understanding that diversity of thought is required for a company to remain competitive. The research shows that teams outperform individual decision makers 66 percent of the time. And if you make that team more diverse, if it includes different ages, genders, and geographic locations, that percentage rises to 87 percent. A 2015 report by the management consultancy firm McKinsey & Company found that the companies who had the most ethnic and racial diversity in management were 35 percent more likely to have higher financial returns. A *Harvard Business Review* piece said, "In recent years a body of research has revealed another, more nuanced benefit of workplace diversity: nonhomogenous teams are simply smarter."

Diversity and inclusion are highly valued by organizations such as Deloitte and the NFL. The wisdom of having different voices at the table makes great sense when you look at what happened with a now-infamous Pepsi commercial. In the commercial, model and reality star Kendall Jenner spontaneously joins a protest march, grabbing a Pepsi from a well-stocked cooler as she engages in what seems more like merriment than activism. Then she hands a Pepsi to a police officer at the front of the barrier. The public outcry about the ad was immediate, as it was, simply, tone-deaf. It didn't reflect or honor the real nature and sacrifice of protest in America. Pepsi took down the ad and wrote in a public apology that "Pepsi was trying to project a global message of unity, peace, and understanding. Clearly we missed the mark, and we apologize." Gucci and H&M both recently made racially insensitive blunders: the former when it marketed a wool sweater that pulls up over the bottom of the wearer's face and looks a whole lot like blackface, and the latter when it featured a photo of an African American kid wearing a sweatshirt that read *Coolest monkey in the jungle*. Diversity and inclusion problems are everywhere—universities, entertainment, banking, the arts. Lack of representation at the decision-making levels plagues these industries, thus allowing biases to be carried through to the end. In the case of the fashion industry, the items weren't vetted, and the right people weren't in the room to point out how offensive the clothing designs were.

How does this happen? Remember again the study I cited at the beginning of this chapter, of people who would rather earn less money than read about another point of view. Participants didn't want to hear the opposing position and felt that doing so "'would create cognitive dissonance'—the psychological discomfort that arises from simultaneously holding two opposing beliefs." But the fact is that we cannot be strong negotiators unless we stretch ourselves.

The more you learn, the more you know

After all of the preparation before a negotiation comes the encounter itself, the phase where you will exchange information with your counterpart. You're not jumping right into bargaining, even if the encounter is over the phone. Instead, exchanging information requires that you take your time to get to know each other. It could be that something you learn about the person affects how you will approach the negotiation—you have to be prepared to waver from whatever script you've come with. It's the same principle as a science experiment: Make a hypothesis, test it, and adjust. If you find that your assumptions are wrong, you don't need to abandon your goals. But you may need to find a different way to get there or modify your goal to reflect the new information that was introduced in the conversation. Perhaps you learn that a toy you wanted to buy for your child is in higher demand than you anticipated before you went into a store. Your interest is still the same—you want that toy—but you have to look at your budget more creatively, or look at the used market, now that you know more about the toy's limited supply. It's akin to driving down the highway to find that your exit's been closed. You still want to be committed to your desired outcome, but you remain flexible about other ways of arriving there. You may even be surprised to find a better way.

Always stay in fact-finding mode instead of feeling beholden to a script. Choose curiosity over certainty. As Leo Tolstoy wrote in *The Kingdom of God Is Within You*, "The most difficult subjects can be explained to the most slow-witted man if he has not formed any idea of them already; but the simplest thing cannot be made clear to the most intelligent man if he is firmly persuaded that he knows already, without a shadow of a doubt, what is laid before him."

Information exchange involves asking questions, showing authentic interest in your counterpart, and creating a natural rapport that puts both sides at ease. I always think of the information exchange that happens before an opening offer as "pure"—you're curious about your counterpart and want to know more about them and everything that may affect the deal in some way. Information exchange takes time—but take the time you need. The more you learn before initiating the actual bargaining process, the more likely you are to engage in a negotiation that is thoughtful, consensus-driven (because you have successfully established an understanding of your mutual interests), and void of derailing surprises. In other words, by the time of the opening offer, you've already done most of the work. But information exchange does not stop once someone has thrown out an opening offer—you never close the door to learning more. Once the opening offer is made, though, the learning isn't as pure. You're learning with the opening offer firmly ingrained in the back of your mind, offering a backdrop to the discussion.

Even if you agree, in theory, that spending time exchanging

information is worth the time, the work has just begun. This is the art of conversation, and it's not easy. If you do it incorrectly, your counterpart may feel like they're being interrogated or interviewed for a job. But the more you engage in conversations and ask open-ended questions, the better you become at making authentic connections—which is very different from thinking, *Okay, I need to get through a few minutes of frivolous small talk and then we can get to business.* The better you become at conversation, the more you see it's not frivolous at all. *Fresh Air* host Terry Gross—who has made a brilliant career out of being a skilled conversationalist—told the *New York Times* that "Tell me about yourself" is possibly the most powerful way to open any conversation. It doesn't make presumptions, the way "What do you do for work?" does, and it lets your companion begin the conversation where they want to. Plus, people on the whole *like* talking about themselves!

You don't want your counterpart to feel you're asking questions in order to manipulate them; your curiosity must be genuine. If you ask a question, even one as basic as, "Where did you go on vacation last summer?" you have to care to listen to the answer. Don't ask questions about a subject that's not meaningful to you. Dale Carnegie wrote: "The difference between appreciation and flattery? That is simple. One is sincere and the other insincere. One comes from the heart out; the other from the teeth out. One is unselfish; the other selfish. One is universally admired; the other universally condemned."

If this whole line of reasoning is making you squirm because you hate small talk, know that I get it. So do I. I'm an introvert who goes to receptions all the time and my first thought, when looking around the room of mostly strangers, is that I want to pull out my phone and check emails, sports scores, or the news. I don't want to chat with someone just because.

I'm not suggesting, then, that you force yourself to become an extrovert. It would feel disingenuous if I suddenly strived to be the center of attention at a party of strangers. Instead, I channel the part of myself that is genuinely curious about other people. I've noticed that the most amazing thing happens when I decide I'm going to be curious for just a little while before I go back to my cave of sports scores and news. Let's say I see a woman who it doesn't look like I have a lot in common with, but she's wearing shoes that are to die for. I admit that I'm a shoeaholic, so when I say something to her about them, it's genuine. I can find an angle where I'm authentically interested, and, paired with an intent to be curious, it's remarkable how the conversation flows and how much I learn.

A study out of the University of Rochester showed just how much curiosity like this matters in personal relationships. The study paired participants up and, before putting them into conversation with one another, measured their level of curiosity. The couples were assigned either a small-talk conversation or an intimate conversation. Those who had lower levels of curiosity going into the experiment experienced greater closeness in the intimacy-producing situation but not the small-talk situation. Those who had been judged to have high levels of curiosity, on the other hand, experienced greater closeness with their partner, regardless of the nature of the conversation. In simple terms, they connect with people better. As highly curious individuals have more closeness with their conversation partner, they naturally acquire more knowledge about that individual, which leads to more creative solutions.

Sarah Farzam, founder of Bilingual Birdies, used to dread meetings that involved negotiation. Then she realized that she loved meeting people and she loved hearing their stories. If she made this her focus, she looked forward to it. You may recall that Sarah is Jewish, Mexican, and Iranian. She speaks four languages and the entire point of her business is to help children appreciate other cultures.

"I'm genuinely interested in people," Sarah said, so it's natural for her to ask questions. "I'll ask, 'So how long have you been working here? I see your last name is Martinez—do you speak Spanish? Tell me about that.' They tell me their stories and all about their family and where they come from. Everyone is at some point an immigrant."

How Sarah enters those conversations depends on what she knows about her counterpart's culture. When she is negotiating with someone from a Middle Eastern culture, for example, she makes it all about the relationship. "I try to make the conversation an experience. In Iranian culture, for instance, people come to your house and they roll out the red carpet for you. They're not going to give you three pieces of food and that's it. They're going to bring people to *sing* for you. So I try to re-create that. I say, 'Let's get the chai. Let's talk.'" She plays up the part of her own personality that will show she relates.

"It makes sense to do," she said of the information-gathering she prioritizes, "because (a) it's genuine, (b) people like it, and (c) I like it. Even if I don't get a deal, I feel like I've learned so much."

Sarah is unabashedly curious. Curious negotiators notice everything and treat negotiation just as sommeliers approach wine. You don't use just a single sense as a sommelier; you don't ask, "White or red?" You take your time, you think about smell and food pairings and the process that went into making the wine you recommend. You listen for understanding, not for validation of what you already have assumed. As the Dalai Lama said, "When you talk, you are only repeating what you already know. But if you listen, you may learn something new."

Becoming genuinely interested in people

Information exchange is particularly easy to skip over with family members, because we think we know everything there is to know about them. But that's not always the case—in fact, it's *usually* not the case. My friend Emma told me that information exchange had dramatically improved her marriage. She and her husband continuously argued about how to discipline their children. She felt her husband was too lenient, and he thought she was too strict. It panicked him whenever she raised her voice to one of the kids, and he grew frantic if she even suggested the prospect of spanking. She'd been brought up in a household where spanking was acceptable. Her parents hadn't done it a lot, but for offenses that were alarming—like disrespect—they had felt it was an appropriate way to send a message, and she agreed. She and her husband constantly butted heads until she decided to apply the concepts of curiosity to their next negotiation about discipline. Instead of fighting about the fact that they felt differently, she wanted to understand *why* they felt differently. What values had her husband grown up with that made him feel so strongly? She asked him question after question. Only after they had been talking about it for some time did he reveal that he had been physically abused as a child. She had been with her husband for over a decade and had never known. Now that she did, it changed everything, brought them closer, and offered a new framing for some of their most perpetual arguments.

My friend Joan called me seething after she got home from a morning workout to find a sink full of dishes and an unemptied but clean dishwasher while her husband was on the computer upstairs. She and her husband were in a rush to get out of town and had a dogsitter staying. Joan figured her husband had probably just expected her to do the dishes. And he was also being passive-aggressive, she thought, mad that she'd gone to work out. She called me as she angrily put dishes away. She was ready to bite her husband's head off. This was a negotiation in the making, and it had the potential to go very badly. So I encouraged Joan to think of it the way she would any professional negotiation. The first thing she needed to do was show curiosity. She should ask her husband—and not in an accusatory way—why he hadn't done the dishes. She should be genuine in her desire to know his thought process without judgment.

Joan took my advice and, instead of launching into accusations, asked her husband nonconfrontational questions and committed to listening. What had he been doing? Had he been in the kitchen? As it turned out, he'd been working on a home loan for them that had a tight turnaround. He had seen the dishes, but he hadn't expected Joan to do them. Rather, he thought it was fair for them to expect the dogsitter to do them since there were only a few and, from his point of view, they were paying her an excellent rate to basically snuggle their dog for a couple of days.

There was still a conflict here—Joan felt the dishes should be done before they left, and her husband didn't. But now that they'd worked out each of their interests, the couple could focus the conversation on the question that was really at hand: What is a reasonable expectation for a dogsitter?

Similarly, James and his wife were looking for a family home to buy and couldn't agree on a place to make an offer. What's more, when they discussed different houses, they'd start to argue. "I travel a lot," James explained, "so the house is not as important to me. I was looking at the bottom line." His wife, who stayed home with the kids, was looking for what would be best for them, where they would play, which neighborhoods made sense. "She kept finding places that were over budget, and I found places that weren't considerate of her needs. We were being dismissive of each other." When James decided to focus on being curious, the conversation went much better. "We had a discussion about another house. And instead of dismissing it, I became more specific about why I didn't like it. Then [my wife] said that she cared a lot about the neighborhood for all of these reasons, but that she's willing to sacrifice something else. Because we were explaining what we really wanted instead of just saying, 'I want this and she wants that,' we were willing to bend. We understood where the other one was coming from, and we both wanted to please the other because we love each other." When they were going to bed that night, James's wife said, "That is the best conversation we have had in some time."

In my final (and probably favorite) story of how families can practice open-mindedness with one another, my former student Michael was in a really awkward place. His wife asked him to talk to her father about a complicated family negotiation that had reached deadlock. "I'm a chiropractor who took a negotiations class," Michael reminded her. "I'm not sure I have a lot to offer here." But he agreed to try.

Their predicament was fraught, to say the least. It all started when Michael and his wife, Susan, wanted to buy a home in San Francisco, and Michael's father-in-law, Jack, agreed to pay half, on the condition that the house would be put in a trust for the grandchildren. Michael and Susan agreed, and after the purchase of the home, they hired an attorney who specialized in trusts to draw it up. Jack asked to see the trust and was not happy that *he* wasn't the sole trustee. How was he to be 100 percent confident that Michael wouldn't run off with the money? Now, keep in mind that Jack had known Michael since the latter was a little boy. Michael had been married to Jack's daughter for fifteen years, he had three children with her, and their marriage was strong, as was Jack's personal relationship with Michael. Jack's request was unreasonable and insulting. If Michael and Susan ever did divorce, Jack's demand would require Michael to continue paying the mortgage on the home without living there. Because the mortgage was so high, Michael wouldn't have been able to afford another place to live. Jack and Susan had screaming matches over the issue, and because father and daughter were getting nowhere, Michael got involved.

"I knew I couldn't approach it as 'This is my father-in-law giving me a gift,'" he said, nor could he look at it as his father-in-law wishing him harm. "I had to approach it as 'This is someone going in on buying a property with me. How can we make it work?'" When Michael and Jack finally talked about it—in front of Susan and Michael's mother-in-law—Jack expected Michael to be as emotional as Susan had been. "I think Jack was prepared to say, 'I love you like a son, but this is business,'" Michael said, but Jack never needed to say it because Michael didn't get upset. He was calm, and he was focused on being curious about what drove his father-in-law to do the things he did. What was the man's interest?

"Was Jack wanting to be a terrible person?" Michael asked himself. "No. He had a certain interest and wasn't going about getting it in the right way. To this man, the dollar is king. Money is everything. It's very different than in my family, where my mother gave me a check on my wedding day and asked no questions. She wanted to give me a gift, so she gave me a gift. Jack was different. So I had to approach it from a point of view of 'Why do you want this? What is your concern here? What are you worried about me doing?'"

When asked these questions, Jack responded, "I'm worried that if you get divorced and the house gets sold, you'd buy something for yourself with the money."

"Okay," Michael said, still unaffected by the insinuation of this statement. "What if we were to say that if the house gets sold because of divorce, the money still goes to the kids?"

Jack had to agree that this resolved his fear, mostly. But Jack said he was still worried about Michael running off. Then Michael pointed out that there was risk in everything, that they would never get to a place of zero percent risk. "Can I steal the money? Yes, but then the trust would have to come after me. You can't prevent someone from murdering someone else, you can only come after them." Michael helped his father-in-law see how he was overreaching, and they found common ground and, ultimately, an agreement.

It all worked out, but the tension leading up to it could have been avoided. We're not as curious with family members as we should be. We assume we know not only what they think but why they think that way. Susan and Jack clashed for this very reason. But this dynamic keeps us from fact-finding mode, a mode from which we can either validate or dismiss our assumptions.

The impact of perspective

There's a haunting series on Showtime called *The Affair* that begins by exploring an extramarital affair from multiple viewpoints, showing how the same interactions are viewed differently depending on the character. None of the characters are lying, but they are subject to memory bias. Their experience is their experience. You see, for instance, how the married father of four, Noah, sees the younger Alison as flirty and the instigator of their affair. The viewers also see how Alison sees herself very differently and views Noah as the one who came on to her. It's fascinating, from an audience perspective, to see how starkly people "miss" one another as they pass. What's true in this television drama is also true in negotiation.

Your perspective and that of your counterpart can be vastly different, while each of you views the same perceived facts. A few years ago, the issue of perspective elevated to an international frenzy and captivated millions when a wedding guest posted a photo of the mother of the bride wearing a dress that some viewers swore was white and gold while others said it was clearly black and blue. Scientists disagreed about what accounted for the discrepancy, but perspective was clearly at the heart of it. Dr. Duje Tadin, an associate professor of brain and cognitive sciences at the University of Rochester, pointed to variations of photoreceptors in our retinas, and told the *New York Times*, "This clearly has to do with individual differences in how we perceive the world. There's something about this particular image that just captures those differences in a remarkable way."

TV dramas and social media may have a way of creatively capturing these perspective shifts, but it's nothing new. Consider this from nineteenth-century philosopher William James: "Whenever two people meet there are really six people present. There is each man as he sees himself, each man as the other sees him, and each man as he really is." The storylines are endless.

Imagine, then, the power you would have if you didn't insist the dress was blue and black but had the ability to also see it as white and gold. You could make an argument for one perspective while also clearly seeing the other. With this power in hand, you enter another league of negotiator, one where you can more easily broker deals, resolve arguments, and even usher in peace. With this power in hand, you can see new solutions, and tap into generosity. But it isn't easy.

CHAPTER 6

the power of empathy

Once you've learned everything you possibly can about your counterpart and opened yourself up to their point of view, you have to go a step further yet. You can't just read about and ask questions of the other side—you have to actually be able to see things from their perspective, to empathize. You have to be like a Method actor, figuratively walking in their shoes so that you can not only see where they're coming from but respect it, even if you disagree.

Nelson Mandela is perhaps the best modern example of an empathetic negotiator. When he was imprisoned, he learned Afrikaans, the language of his jailers, so as to better understand them. When he was released and elected president, his predecessor, the Afrikaner F. W. de Klerk, served as his vice president. And once when he was berated on the radio by an angry Afrikaner, he said, "Well, Eddie, I regard you as a worthy South African, and I have no doubt that if we were to sit down and exchange views I will come closer to you and you will come closer to me. Let's talk, Eddie." Mandela was considered a "giant of empathy," which was critical to his effective diplomacy.

Empathy isn't a "nice-to-have" for an effective negotiator; it's a must-have. Empathy is a strategic way for you to understand your counterpart that allows you to communicate well. Further, if you don't truly understand where your counterpart is coming from, how do you know how to compromise? How do you know where to make concessions that will really matter to them? Empathy allows for conflict mitigation—that easing of tension, that turning down of the temperature in a potentially heated discussion.

The celebrated hostage negotiator Lt. Jack Cambria prizes empathy as a critical negotiation tool. Now retired from the New York Police Department, he has also trained other negotiators and is considered a bit of a godfather in the business. He told the *Wall Street Journal* that when he is looking for someone to *be* a hostage negotiator, he thinks they must "experience the emotion of love at one point in their life, to know what it means to have been hurt in love at one point in their life, to know success and perhaps, most important, to know what it means to know failure." The hostage takers have demands—but the demands are less important than your having empathy, understanding their emotional state, and connecting with them on that level. Their demands are their wants, but their needs are more emotional and deeper. Former FBI chief negotiator Gary Noesner reflected, "When I used to interview people when they had surrendered after an incident and ask them what one thing I said to make them change their mind, they would invariably reply, 'I don't know what you said but I liked the way you said it.' Our genuine, sincere, and concerned tone and demeanor are the most powerful tools of influence that we know."

Noesner says that when the FBI was working out how to posi-
tively influence people they were negotiating with, they looked to
the writing and research of Robert Cialdini, particularly his book
Influence: The Psychology of Persuasion, which has also been a seminal
text for me. They learned that influence "is all about relationship
building, earning trust and demonstrating a genuine interest in
their issues and concerns. We learned that negotiators needed to
come across as being non-threatening and non-judgmental."

When we seek to empathize, we get closer to resolution . . . even
if it's just marginally so. On a trip to the Middle East during his
presidency, Barack Obama met with a group of Palestinian youth.
According to Obama aide Ben Rhodes, the Palestinians told stories
of having friends imprisoned and the freedom of their movements
restricted. One of the speakers told Obama, "Mr. President, we are
treated the same way the black people were treated in your country.
Here, in this century. Funded by your government, Mr. President."

Shortly afterward, Obama spoke at a conference in Jerusalem.
Although Obama had prepared remarks, at one point he stopped
and said, "I'm going to go off script here for a second, but before I
came here I met with a group of young Palestinians from the age
of fifteen to twenty-two. And talking to them, they weren't that different from my daughters. They weren't that different from your
daughters or sons. I honestly believe that if any Israeli parent sat
down with those kids, they'd say I want these kids to succeed; I want
them to prosper. I want them to have opportunities just like my kids
do. I believe that's what Israeli parents would want for these kids if
they had a chance to listen to them and talk to them. I believe that."
Although Obama could not fix the deep fissures between Israel and
Palestine, he could encourage empathy, just as the Palestinian
speaker had done with Obama.

How empathy translates

Empathy is invaluable in politics and world affairs, and it's also imperative on the smallest scale: that between two family members. Parents, for instance, can turn to empathy when locked in battle with their kids. I remember when one of my nephews was obsessed with gaming. Most of the adults in his life spent most of their energy fighting with him to stop "wasting" so much time instead of stopping to understand why he felt so compelled to spend so many hours gaming in the first place. What was it about gaming that he found so exciting and engaging? The adults in his life, including me, should have put ourselves in his shoes and tried to understand why he felt it was worth so much of his time and energy. We might have learned that he loved gaming because he played with his best friends, and it was the connection to his friends that he most valued. Or we might have learned that it was something he felt he could excel in and master, thus giving him a sense of accomplishment. The truth is I don't know if we ever really understood his motives; we spent so much time being worried about him that every time it came up, we appeared unreasonably protective or judgmental.

Nothing about this conflict is unique to my family. Parents worry about their kids and often feel they just know better, so why not just attempt to stop the activity? This approach rarely works because it doesn't allow for true empathy, for the chance to understand the decisions or actions from the perspective of your child. Without empathy, you appear judgmental, punitive, and unjust. You form barriers to communication and perpetuate misunderstandings.

Many a parent has been in conflict with a surly child who, for whatever reason, is demanding something. Before the parent refuses, they would do well to stop a moment and imagine what's going on with their child. What was their day like that day? How might they be feeling? Is the issue really whatever it is they're demanding, or is it something else?

This tactic isn't only confined to parents, by the way, and I've found it enormously useful as a daughter. In Chapter 2, I wrote about my relationship with my parents, focusing on how it took me a long time to separate their wishes for me from what I authentically wanted. (I suspect I'm not the first child of immigrants to experience this dynamic.) I was angry with them, particularly my father, for insisting that I study medicine instead of seeing that I had no interest in being a doctor. For many years I could not see his perspective. But I eventually came to understand where he was coming from, in a genuine, empathetic way, and not because he told me explicitly but because I worked hard at putting myself in his shoes. When we left Iran, we left everything we knew, everything that defined us. He had been stable and grounded—when he moved us to the United States, the rug was pulled out from under him and stability was no more. He went from being an engineer and managing thousands of people at sugar refineries to running a small convenience store.

When people come to the United States from other countries, there are a million ideas in their heads about what America is like. Just to mention a few, Americans have a different way of raising kids, an incredible freedom of choice, a mantra that says, "Live your dreams! Be what you want to be!" For someone like my dad, this was confusing, undoubtedly scary, and yet he felt he must keep a sense of balance. But how? How could he ensure that the person he was betting the farm on (me!) was successful? How could he make sure I stayed on the right course when there were so many unknowns, including language, culture, and social values? All he felt he could do to protect me was to write the script for my life and tell me to follow it.

The way that my dad pressured me to follow a career path he felt sure to be successful was the way he showed his love for me. Everybody loves differently, and everybody accepts love differently. I wanted a different kind of love from my dad—a kind that was more tactile, unconditional, and nonjudgmental. But because I didn't get it in that way didn't mean it wasn't there. I didn't agree with my father's approach, but working hard to see the world the way he does has been crucial to my capacity to forgive him.

My student Dom told me that the evening after one of our classes where we discussed the importance of empathy in bargaining, he got a chance to try it out. The negotiation, in this case, was with his wife. A group of Dom's friends were getting together, and Dom wanted to go. But he had been out the previous two evenings because of work engagements, and his wife had been left home as the sole parent to their kids. Their discussion about how he would spend his evening was not going well. He kept repeating that he really wanted to go and she kept saying no.

Then he took a step back and tried to empathize. His wife was tired of solo parenting, which he respected. She also was in need of a little love and attention from her husband. Dom owned three businesses and was constantly working—and that clearly made her feel overlooked sometimes. Dom understood then that his wife would respond better to whatever he asked—whether it was that night or the next week—if he could fill up her emotional bank account. So that was what he decided to do.

"You're right," he said. "Let's spend time together this evening. What do you want to do? Do you want to watch a movie or something?" He told her how much he loved and appreciated her and that it was really wonderful to spend time with her. Importantly, all of these statements were true! He felt them all the time, he just was hyperaware that she needed to hear them. He knew it was a possibility that once her "bank account" was filled up, she might change her mind and suggest that he go out with his friends, but he also knew that might not happen and he was perfectly happy in that case to be at home.

After a while, though, she turned to him and said, "You know what? I think you should go out with your friends."

Dom was pretty excited about how effective empathy was, and so he used it in his next work negotiation. One of his companies is an auto body shop, and a large part of the work he does is negotiating estimates with insurance adjusters. The very purpose of an insurance adjuster is not to give way to companies like Dom's. In other words, if ever there was a place where the tactic of empathy would fall short, this was it.

Dom worked with one adjuster with whom he habitually clashed. When the adjuster came in to Dom's shop, he was frowning and just generally looked antagonistic. *Okay*, thought Dom, *here goes*. Dom put his arm around him and said, "Listen, dude. I don't want to go on like this anymore. We're here together for the benefit of our customer. We should be able to work together better."

The adjuster shook his head and said, "No, it's nothing about you. I'm just having a bad day."

"Why?" Dom asked. "What's up?"

The adjuster took out a picture of his son and explained that he'd just had an ugly accident.

"Then what are you doing here?" Dom said. "Go home. Go be with your family. We'll talk tomorrow, don't worry."

When the adjuster came in the next day he said, "I really appreciate what you did for me yesterday."

"I have a little boy too," Dom said. "I would do the same thing."

The two spent the next few hours going over the estimate, and as empathy allowed them to be shoulder-to-shoulder, they came to an agreement they both felt good about.

My student John went through a process that closely mirrored Dom's. He'd recently left the military when he took my class at Wharton, and although the military had given him a code of ethics in his negotiation style that was well defined, he hadn't given much thought to the role of empathy in negotiation. He began using some of what we discussed at class at home with his wife, and at gradua- tion his wife came up to me to tell me how much the class had strengthened their marriage. As John explained, they focus a lot more in their conversations on "understanding the why." "Even if we still end up on opposite ends," he said, "we'll say, at least I under- stand how you got to your why, even though I don't agree with you. It's opened up another layer of communication in our marriage."

He's taken these skills into his work at a private equity firm, where he deals exclusively with distressed debt. "If we're a lender on someone's business loan, and the business deteriorates, we know the collateral that we can come after." With his earlier mind-set, he was more likely to focus on the quantitative data without much thought to the humans behind them. He's seen that mind-set used often by his colleagues who have been in the field a long time and who have become jaded. "It's easy to take the approach, 'Hey, pay me this or we're taking that.'" But employing empathy, he said, while harder, leads to better outcomes. "You actually start looking at the people behind the business, and families. These are just busi- ness owners who were trying to make a living and then it ended up going south and they can't pay their debt." He said when you show compassion, you end up working together and discovering variables—like a health crisis—that had an impact on their ability to pay a loan. "We'll find out after the fact that somebody just got ill, and the business kind of just fell away. You can't discern this from financial statements and hundreds of pages of documents. When you're able to understand the why and how they ended up in these situations, it often can drive a better outcome because you have them on board and working with you. No one necessarily has to be right."

Empathy has a bad rap

Many feel that having too much empathy is a weakness—not an asset—in a negotiation. They argue that you have to be emotionless to be effective; otherwise you are apt to concede too much. My students constantly apologize for their empathy, thinking it gets in the way of effective negotiation. But this is dead wrong. Empathetic people are, in fact, some of the best negotiators out there. Empathetic people are the most able to put themselves in their counterparts' position and assess what they might want. Empathetic people are the ultimate information gatherers.

Empathetic negotiators run into problems only when they get so involved in the feelings of others that they cross over to taking on those challenges as their own. As Dom put it, "Empathy is working with others the best you can. Stupidity is giving away the house." I wouldn't call it stupid, but we do get into trouble when we can't separate ourselves emotionally. This is what Emily, the pleaser who was buying a used car in Chapter 2, struggled with when she thought, "Oh, this poor car salesman is going to be late for dinner with his girlfriend and I can't let that happen." These empathetic people aren't able to draw a line, and their decision making is impacted to their detriment. Deeply intertwined with this tendency is that they are not turning their empathy on *themselves*. These negotiators are focused on other people's needs and wants and mistakenly think they can't also focus on their own, that the two are mutually exclusive. What they don't understand is that without taking care of themselves, too, they can't be effective.

I learned this lesson the hard way with my health care consulting practice. When we had to lay people off, it was awful. I empathized with their disappointment and lost many nights of sleep worrying about them. Although I firmly believe this empathy was essential to the collaborative culture that I was trying to establish, I took it too far. I made it my responsibility to fix it by delaying the downsizing, putting unnecessary strain on our already dwindling budget. I took on their strain and internalized it.

Many leaders find themselves walking the same line I walked, struggling with the same question I did: *How do I care about my employees without caring so much that it affects my ability to run the business?* My student Saudia is one such leader. She founded a cleaning service, and most of her employees come from the same demographic as her mother and grandmother: single moms, immigrants, not formally educated, economically vulnerable. Saudia feels a great sense of responsibility to these employees. She remembers how the first time she gave out paychecks, one of her employees literally ran to the Western Union to send money to her mother in Columbia, who would now be able to afford surgery. The benefits and consequences of Saudia's business success feel very personal because they are.

When Saudia realized she had a seriously underperforming employee, she was in a hard spot and went through a grueling negotiation within herself. Letting this employee go would have real consequences. This employee would undoubtedly not go quietly— there would be a conflict. This employee had a family. It was the holidays. Saudia could track the ripple effects of the act. Simply put, no matter what she did, people were going to be pissed. Saudia had to get herself to a place where she could see all the ripples through to their natural ending and still fire the employee. She had to do it, because there were financial consequences to not doing it. She had to do it, because other employees were relying on Saudia to steer the ship. She had to do it, because as much as she wanted to take care of everyone, sometimes as the boss, you can't.

"The internal negotiations [with myself] are the ones that are hardest," Saudia said. She had to give herself permission to use her empathy but not be hobbled by it. She knew she could do it because she'd just had a similar internal negotiation about her nanny.

"I knew my first one wasn't right," she said. "I saw the ripple effect. I knew my child was attached to her. I knew there would be a transition period where I'd need to be at home. I was negotiating the repercussions instead of negotiating the action I needed to do. My significant other will say, 'You have to think about it this way: How much better is it going to be with someone new who is going to be able to do this job effectively?' There are so many plusses that you can't worry about the minuses."

Letting each person go was uncomfortable, as expected, but Saudia knew it was the right call. "I have to constantly remind myself that in all of my thirteen years in business, I have never regretted firing someone. However, I have constantly and consistently regretted not firing someone sooner."

John Lynch, former star NFL safety, works in a very different field, but like Saudia, he uses empathy daily in his work. He knows what it's like to be a young player worried about proving himself. He also knows what it's like to be a veteran player coming to terms with the idea that perhaps it's time to move on. Now he's the general manager of the San Francisco 49ers and sits on the other side of the table. He has to make dozens of fast decisions daily, he said, decisions that affect people's livelihoods and families. A naturally empathetic human being, he has had to work hard at using that trait for the good of the organization.

"A couple of weeks ago," he told me, "we were talking to players who were drafted, and I realize the impact that has on their achieving a dream. I think, I've been there before. I've been a player early in a career where you're drafted, but gosh, do you really believe you can make it? I understand how that feels." When he has to make the tough calls about personnel—which he must do constantly—he uses empathy to inform him how. He or head coach Kyle Shanahan try to meet personally with every player who is let go. "It comes from having been there myself and knowing what I appreciated, someone looking you in the eye. I think it's also important to tell people the truth, saying, 'Hey. Here's why we cut you.' In particular, if they ask questions—'Why me instead of this guy?'—I say, 'Well, I'm not going to get into talking about this guy, but for you, here's what our mindset was.'" The same approach applies when players ask, as they sometimes will, if he thinks it's time for them to move on. "I'm willing to say, 'Hey, I don't know everything, but yeah. I think it might be that time,' because I think that's what I would want to hear and I think having been there helps me in those situations."

Now John is also involved in front-office negotiation, and he uses his experience as a player in that context as well. His ability to understand the players gives him better insight into their interests, their struggles, their fears, and their decision making as a whole. This gives him great advantages when negotiating with agents. He knows their clients and can be better at anticipating their needs and wants. He can also be more effective in framing things for the players from the perspective of the organization so that they can understand the dynamics. In this sense, his empathy can make him more persuasive.

Leaving something on the table

For weeks in 2015, various governments of the world met in Switzerland to solve a stubborn, decadelong stalemate over Iran's nuclear weapons program wherein they ultimately agreed to lift sanctions in return for Iran making concessions to their nuclear program. Many Americans criticized the agreement, feeling that the United States hadn't been tough enough, that we hadn't gotten enough for ourselves out of the deal. Years later, Mohammad Javad Zarif, foreign minister of Iran, made the point that no one was entirely happy with the deal—that's how they knew it was a good deal. "I never believed in zero-sum games," Zarif told CNN's Fareed Zakaria. "We reached a deal that nobody likes. And it's good. Because no good deal is a perfect deal. Because you cannot have a perfect deal for both sides. You need to have a deal that is less than perfect so that both sides can reach an understanding . . . it doesn't have all the things that we wanted in the deal. It doesn't have everything that the U.S. wanted in the deal."

According to a BBC documentary, the environment of the negotiations was more like a dormitory than a summit, where everyone stayed in the same hotel and worked all hours of the day and night against deadlines that came and went. The lead U.S. negotiator, Wendy Sherman, talked about how they sometimes dined with the Iranians, and how important it was to build the relationships. She also talked of how she and Iran's lead negotiator both became grandparents during the course of the negotiations and showed each other videos of their grandchildren. They were human beings to each other, but that didn't mean they weren't tough, too. "He had a responsibility to the national interests of his country, and I had a responsibility to the national interest of my country," she said.

Harnessing the power of empathy often means leaving something on the table, because you try to understand what the other side is dealing with as best you can, and you know what they can sell and what they can't. You make concessions, which isn't about giving ground but more about problem solving: You give up something that's less important to you in order to get something that's more important to you. Making concessions well requires knowing your interest well, as well as really understanding your counterpart's, so that you know what to offer as a concession that will be meaningful.

The practice of leaving something on the table is also known as *win-win* negotiating, but I've always been wary of that moniker because it can be misleading: win-win implies that everyone gets their way, and that's not the case. Rather, win-win means that both parties leave the negotiation feeling better off than they were before they started talking. It may not mean they both got everything they wanted, but they are now more likely to have met their most important interests while conceding things that were not as relevant.

In addition, they feel that the negotiation has gone as well as it could have for *both* parties. Expectations have been managed, such that neither party feels they have come out the loser. Note the use of the word *feel*. Win-win negotiation relies heavily on emotional intelligence, because you have to be aware of how your counterpart interprets and reacts to whatever twists and turns the negotiation takes—and to how your counterpart interprets even a seemingly "easy" negotiation. When a group of researchers studied reactions to opening offers, they found that when those opening offers were accepted right away, the party who offered it felt less satisfied with the agreement. Could they have done better? Did they not ask for enough?

Years ago, sports agent Bob Woolf told *Inc.* that he made it a regular practice to leave money on the table. "It's possible to push the price so far, create such antagonism, that the extra 10% isn't really worth it. If someone feels you held them up, they're going to take it out on your business or—if it's an employee—on you. In my case, they'll take it out on my client, make him miserable, trade him. Obviously, a negotiation isn't about only money." Put another way, you cannot have a satisfying negotiation *without* empathy, because then how could you know that the other side truly feels like they've won too?

Amy Voloshin, cofounder of Printfresh Studio and the Voloshin clothing line, is a rising star in the world of fashion and textiles. In the course of growing her business, she said she realized that "your best-case scenario is where everyone walks away happy." When she is doing salary negotiations, she said, "I can't just send [the candidate] an email. Knowing more about where they're coming from makes it so much easier. Maybe there's a cap to the salary we're offering, but maybe being paid 50k instead of 49k is huge." They're going to be part of her team, she said, and she wants them to walk away feeling like their wants were met and that they're valued. Similarly, Amy has noticed that when they get bids in from vendors, the male-owned firms tend to price themselves higher than female-owned firms. So if they get a quote in from a female-owned firm that's reasonable, while Amy's husband and cofounder would say "always negotiate," Amy disagrees. "His natural tendency is to ask for a better price whereas I'm more apt to say it's a reasonable price." She knows, in her ability to relate to their perspective, that the women are offering what they can do the job for without being squeezed. She doesn't want them to feel underpaid for the job, because then no one wins.

You haven't really succeeded if you get the most money out of the negotiation but your counterpart leaves feeling angry, or cheated, or bitter. What about your future working relationship? What about your reputation? There are real costs here, and even if you did exceptionally well in a negotiation, you want to leave your partner feeling that she did, too.

Concessions, made with empathy, not only are good for the long term but can have immediate impact. Charalambos Vlachoutsicos, a professor in Athens, Greece, believes that the use of empathy saved his business. As he tells it in an article for the *Harvard Business Review*, his company, which was in the business of reselling electrical fixtures, got a quote for the fixtures from a company in India. They then offered the fixtures to their customers for a good price based on that quote. The problem was, the Indian company then said they couldn't honor the quote—in fact, the actual cost was 40 percent *higher*. Vlachoutsicos's company was in a terrible position. Purchasing the fixtures at the price from the Indian company would be a huge loss for them; on the other hand, telling their customers "Sorry, it's actually a lot more than we originally told you" would ruin their credibility.

What were the options? Obviously, one was to scream and shout at the Indian company, which happened. (And got them nowhere.) A lawsuit could have been another option, but international litigation is rarely desirable. Vlachoutsicos chose to pursue a course of understanding and empathy, which he believed would help them work toward a solution they could all live with. He flew to meet with the Indian company in person and used all of the open-minded approaches I covered in the last chapter. He asked them what had happened to make them change their quote, and when they told him that it was an error in their accounting department about the cost of the materials, he realized that they really didn't have any room to budge. He also realized the Indian company didn't recognize what a big loss this screwed-up quote represented for Vlachoutsicos's company. Together, they talked through all of the ramifications, and also the possibilities if they could make the deal work somehow. Not only would this Indian company be able to stay in the Greek market—something that surely would not happen were the whole deal to fall apart—but it was an opportunity for expansion into other European markets. They could look at the deal differently, less as a one-off and more as an investment. Ultimately they came to an arrangement where Vlachoutsicos's company would pay 10 percent more than the quoted price and thereby break even. According to Vlachoutsicos, "the main factor for this successful outcome was the fact that we had genuinely tried to put ourselves in their shoes and realized the big financial loss they would suffer. Our arguments for reducing the price back to where it had been were not based on our interests but rather on an objective analysis of the risks and opportunities they faced." In other words, Vlachoutsicos framed the negotiation based on the *Indian company's* interests. "Moreover," he wrote, "the fact that we did not actually make a profit at the new price was a face-saver for the Indian company as it further demonstrated that both sides were making a sacrifice."

Empathy is simply too valuable to the toolbox of a negotiator— be it a hostage negotiator or a politician like President Obama—to keep its bad rap. My hope is that I never again have a student say, "Professor, I'm not cut out for negotiation because I'm too empathetic." Nope. As long as you are turning your empathy on yourself, too, and looking out for your interests, you should own that empathy for all you can. Better still, use it.

CHAPTER 7

wherever you are, be there fully

When I first started teaching, I didn't think as much about how I would get my points across because my brain was fully occupied with what I needed to say. I also had my fair share of lesson plans from which I was not willing to deviate. Now that I've been teaching for fifteen years, I've let go of all of the rigid rules I set for myself in favor of just being in the moment with my class, and it's shocking to me what it's opened up. I notice everything about my students. In a class of thirty-six or forty-eight students, I notice if someone who is usually smiling isn't. I notice if someone is checking their phone (which they shouldn't be—more on that later). I notice if a student feels uncomfortable or anxious. I find that I'm now able to be incredibly present, curious, and laser-focused on my students at any given moment. I walk into a classroom and immediately take inventory of the mood and energy in the room. I can sense where my students are, mentally and emotionally. For the next three hours, I am only there, in the presence of my students, and give little thought to anything outside the classroom no matter what baggage I was carrying prior to walking in. I leave it all at the door. And I've been told again and again that this presence—some would say intensity—is what makes my classes impactful.

I'm not a meditation expert or a yogi by any stretch (no pun intended) and can more likely be found taking a SoulCycle class or sprinting through a busy airport than sitting on a yoga mat. But I firmly believe that cultivating presence is one of the best things we can do to find satisfaction in our day-to-day experiences, improve our relationships, and succeed in negotiations. You cannot be open-minded or empathetic without presence, because the three are so closely intertwined. When we are distracted, we are unable to notice people, emotions, reactions, and our surroundings. When we're distracted we get our information not in totality but through a filter. This is detrimental in negotiation, because negotiation relies on the art of noticing *everything*.

Without being present, you are unable to tap into your emotional intelligence, or EQ, as it's often called, and truly understand the state of mind of your counterpart. This emotional intelligence is a superpower in a negotiation, and distraction is like kryptonite. Sometimes the most important information someone tells you is what they aren't saying at all. A smile, a frown, shifting uncomfortably in their seat, nodding yes when they are saying no: You have to be fully present to capture these nuanced cues as part of the big picture.

Without being present, you cannot recognize when you're becoming tense, or nervous, or angry. Without being present you don't know when to take that break to calm your nervous system so that you don't say something you regret and possibly blow the deal.

Without being present, you may not be aware of signals that your body is bringing into the conversation of its own accord . . . that you're nervously tapping your pen, that your voice is sharp, that your face is flushed.

Ambassador Wendy Sherman negotiated on behalf of the United States at the highest levels, and says she noticed everything about her counterpart, Iranian foreign minister Javad Zarif. "Over time I learned to tell which of Zarif's dramatic turns were for effect and which meant he was truly upset," she wrote in her book about the experience, "and thus whether I should strike a conciliatory tone by addressing him as 'Javad' or call him 'Minister,' by which he would know that I was ticked off and not buying his dramatics."

It's powerful to notice that glance, that smile, that uncomfort-able movement. As negotiation scholar Max Bazerman put it, "What's in front of you is rarely all there is." So you have to learn to truly *see*. My students who are distracted lose information, so they can't gain leverage. But to focus takes concentration and stamina. Most people have an attention span of approximately eight seconds, il-lustrating that we're more distractible than goldfish. We don't give enough credence to the notion that being present is *hard*.

It's only gotten harder, thanks to a hyperconnected world where multitasking is the de facto way of being. We don't connect as mean-ingfully with one another when we're texting over a meal or doing two things at once in any context. We miss the cues from our friends and loved ones that might tell us more about their state of mind.

As with so many other companies, Mary Ellen Slayter's market-ing company does a lot of its business over email. She said, "A lot of what I do is based on having to read people over the phone and read-ing intent in emails. Any chance I get to see someone in person, especially the higher the stakes it is, I go. I try to get as much information and I don't look at my phone and I don't do other things. I need to take it in . . . because most of the decisions [my clients make], even though they're big corporate decisions, they're ultimately personal decisions and I need the best read on their emotional state as I can get."

Teaching this in my classes has reinforced presence for me, and I work at it every day. When I teach, I try to send a message to my students that there is no place more important than where I am at that moment and no conversation more critical than the one I am having. I've noticed that as a result, I'm better able to meet my students where they are, to respond to them, and to couch the information in a way that I know they will hear it. I believe that level of presence is the ultimate sign of respect and allows me to demand the same in return.

I've also made a point of practicing presence on the journey to and from the classroom. I ride in Ubers and taxis all the time, and one goal I've set is to keep my phone in my bag, and my mind and body in the present for the duration of the journey. In full disclosure, this goal actually began because I wanted to raise my rating from Uber drivers, and I learned they hate it when riders spend the whole time either talking on or looking at their phones. I know, the competitive side of me rears its head more often than not. But what started as a game turned into a breakthrough. I found I love my time on the road. I'll chat with the drivers about where they're from and what their lives are like. I'll look out the window, and often notice buildings I've never noticed before. I once asked my driver if a building in my neighborhood was new. Turns out I'd just not looked at it before. I've started asking the drivers to take a scenic route to get to the train station, so that in between rushing to get out of the house and rushing through the train station, I have time to process, transition, and just stare out the window. Should someone try to reach me during this time, I won't answer my phone, or I'll tell them I can't talk because I'm rushing to catch my train. It's partly true—I *am* en route to Union Station. But the full truth is that I treasure this period of just being.

I've adopted a similar practice on airplanes. Instead of immediately opening my computer or taking out my book, I look out the window whenever there's a sunrise or a sunset. The fact that I fly all the time has gone from being an annoyance to being a gift. When I look out the window of an airplane, I appreciate it, I find peace in it, and I find gratitude in it. People around me must think it's my first time flying, because I'm so captured by the scenery outside. Little do they know I've got elite status on three different airlines and Amtrak. I'm just captivated because I've learned to cultivate presence and gratitude for the moments of stillness in an otherwise crazy busy life.

I was so grateful for this habit when, after a recent week of rushing around nonstop, I boarded a flight to teach a class in Providence. When the plane doors shut and I collected myself and took a breath, I almost immediately realized that I wasn't supposed to teach in Providence that day. Had I not stopped to take that breath but immediately plowed into emails, I might not have recognized my mistake at all and would have gone all the way to the class site.

What could have been a day filled with frustration and self-blaming was, in actuality, a really nice day. I chalked it up to a lesson—an expensive one, but still—about how I need to get off the hamster wheel more often and slow down. I considered the time a gift to myself. I realized that being angry and frustrated wouldn't help. I let the mistake go and calmly talked to the gate agents in Providence, who immediately put me on the next flight out without hesitation and gave me an upgraded seat as well. I didn't even try to access the flights' wireless service. Instead I spent the time to and from Providence reading magazines that I never get a chance to read, planning my week, sipping drinks, and enjoying a few hours to reset. It was a beautiful day to fly, and I spent a good part of the time just looking out the window.

In this chapter, I cover why it's hard to be present, and why it's so important. Yes, technology is a huge distractor, and I'll get into that, but the smartphone is not the only difficulty we face. It turns out that it is very difficult to listen—and I mean *really* listen—without thinking about what you are going to say next, or without any sort of agenda, and yet true presence requires this mindful listening. It's also difficult to be mindful about not just what your words are communicating but what your body language is projecting and what story your facial expressions are revealing. Often they are not in sync. Finally, I'll cover ways to plan for and manage your emotions in a negotiation, whether it's a heated discussion with a family member or a business deal that keeps you up at night.

Free to be phone-free

When the Obamas hosted their final party at the White House, I was fortunate enough to get an invitation, and I brought my oldest nephew as my plus-one. When we got to the security check-in, my nephew learned that we would have to leave our phones before we entered. My nephew was distraught, to say the least. "This is the worst thing ever," he said. "No one will believe I was here." Ever the realist, I pointed out there wasn't really anything he could do about it. So we took a quick photo where we stood outside, left our phones behind, and went in.

It was a spectacular, star-studded evening. The evening started with performances from Usher, the Roots, De La Soul, Jill Scott, and others. The afterparty felt otherworldly, where the likes of Dave Chappelle and Bradley Cooper were just hanging out in the comfort of their peers and free from cell phones and paparazzi. Even though my nephew fought it at first because he was being uncharacteristically shy, I introduced him to Dave Chappelle and they had the chance to share their mutual admiration for the Golden State Warriors. I was for sure up for the Aunt of the Year Award. Music blasted in the background, food and drink were abundant, and we all enjoyed what we knew was one of the highlights of our lives. We didn't leave until after two a.m. On the way home, my nephew said, "I'm so glad I couldn't use my phone. I just had one of the best nights of my life and I actually got to experience it."

We're so caught up in Instagram that we're pulled away from the actual moment. We *think* we're experiencing it, but we're somewhere else, viewing it through a filter. Because my nephew didn't have his phone, he got to see the performances, hear the music, and really take in that once-in-a-lifetime event. For the first time in a long time, he felt what it was like to be fully present. Although I'm an avid social media user as well, I much prefer "post-a-gram" to Instagram, where I take a few pictures to capture a moment and, later, when I have time and am reliving the memory, I post on Instagram or Facebook. It's a walk down memory lane as opposed to robbing myself of the joy of that memory in that moment.

My classes are technology-free zones. No laptops, no phones, no tablets, and even no smart watches. I think of my classroom as a laboratory where we emulate the behaviors that we should practice in any negotiation outside the classroom. Therefore, I want my students to experience being present. If your phone is in your line of sight, vibrating in your pocket, or even if you're immersed in typing notes on what the other party is saying, you're probably missing cues that being more aware would provide you. Research backs me up on this: A 2017 study showed that the mere presence of your phone is distracting—even if you're not paying attention to it, even if it's in airplane mode, even if it's powered off. Because we now rely on our phones for so much, it's like they're calling to us: "Pick me up! Just one quick look!" You may be listening with your ears, but you're not really hearing. Or maybe you're hearing, but you're not gaining valuable information by watching. Worse yet, you might be signaling to the other party that you don't care what they're saying.

Some of my students push back. Those in the Goldman Sachs 10,000 Small Businesses classes are accustomed to being glued to their phones 24/7. Since they are running a business while attending the program, they multitask all the time—they feel they have to. Some students will be surreptitious, checking their phones when they think I'm not looking. But in part because I've completely separated myself from all of my devices, I notice *everything*, so they always get caught. It doesn't matter how many times I say it, there's rarely a time when a student doesn't reach for their phone or forgets to put it away. Sometimes I feel like this is the hardest thing I teach!

Other students nod when I make the request and say they get it. They've heard a lot about mindfulness, maybe even read some articles and studies. But they are as plugged in to their phones as everyone else. A 2018 study of two thousand Americans showed that they checked their phones an average of every twelve minutes *while on vacation*. Feel the sun, hear the surf, breathe in the wind, then check your email. There's something wrong with this picture, and we all know it. My students are willing to give putting their phones down a try, though, because intellectually they buy in. But they don't fully buy in until they see what a difference presence makes for themselves.

"I have such a major problem with my phone," said my student James, for whom the no-cell-phone rule was challenging. He feels he needs to always be in contact with his office. "It causes me anxiety because I'm so super connected. It makes me half-present in connections with human beings." He has two children, ages three and six, and he said that when he takes them to the park, "They'll play on the playground and I'm checking my phone and sending emails. And I'm checking things that could wait an hour or two. It's just such an addiction." He felt what a difference it made in class when he was forbidden to use his phone, and how he had a different level of engagement with whomever he was talking with. At the same time, maintaining that level of engagement with others was tiring and led him to recognize how his attention span has gone down. "I'm used to being on the phone and bouncing from one thing to the other," he said, noting that he doesn't even read anymore.

He's not unusual. Maryanne Wolf is a scientist who has researched reading and the brain and documented her findings first in the book *Proust and the Squid*, then in *Reader, Come Home: The Reading Brain in a Digital World*. In the latter she writes, "Perhaps you have already noticed how the quality of your attention has changed the more you read on screens and digital devices. Perhaps you have felt a pang of something subtle that is missing when you seek to immerse yourself in a once favorite book. Like a phantom limb, you remember who you were as a reader, but cannot summon that 'attentive ghost' with the joy you once felt in being transported somewhere outside the self to that interior space."

I've noticed that it takes me all day to read the newspaper on Sundays. It didn't use to be that way—I used to read the paper edition of the Sunday *New York Times* cover to cover in just a couple of hours. I'd be done in plenty of time to watch football for the rest of the day. Now I find that my attention won't hold for the two hours it used to take—my mind bounces around all over the place—and I'm still reading parts of the paper during the Sunday-night game. It's not ideal, but I'm grateful that I'm at least aware of it.

When it comes to negotiation, the implications of our loss of attention are huge. In an exchange that is so common I can't even attach it to a specific class or exercise, I'll debrief a negotiation with my students and it will become clear that some missed key information in the printed case study. There's a famous negotiation exercise, for instance, that revolves around an orange. There are different adaptations of the exercise—in Roger Fisher's classic book *Getting to Yes*, it involves two kids who both want the last orange in the fruit bowl, whereas in other adaptations it involves two companies who want a rare orange to develop lifesaving products. But one party needs only the rind (in the case of the kids, for baking), whereas the other party needs only the pulp. If you read the description of a case too quickly, you can miss this key information.

I tell my students who make this mistake: "Why didn't you just negotiate for the rind? You didn't need the rest," to which they argue, "I needed the whole thing. Not just the rind."

"Fourteen years later," I tease, reminding them how many times I have seen this exercise, "I think I know."

"No," they say with complete certainty, "it doesn't say that on *my* sheet." Sometimes, it's not until I physically circle it for them in pen on *their* sheet that they see what they missed.

Whatever I say from there on out about presence is taken much more seriously. Little by little, negotiation by negotiation, they see how much being distracted hurts them. And how being distracted is likely the norm, and being present is an exception.

Negotiations are all about relationships and connection. If you believe that's important and then simultaneously you're on your phone, or you're distracted, you're negating that connection. In Chapter 6, I wrote about how empathy is critical to negotiation. But technology may actually lower empathy, according to research. Sherry Turkle is a research psychologist at MIT and author of *Reclaiming Conversation*. She says that we learn intimacy and empathy through conversation and through face-to-face interaction. When we're on our screens instead, we miss out on that. It makes sense. How can we recognize the slight crinkle in a forehead that signals concern if we stop learning to read facial expressions and only read emoticons?

Mary Ellen Slayter, my Goldman Sachs 10,000 Small Businesses program student whose content marketing company is on fire, took these lessons to heart and felt a huge shift in her negotiations. Although in her preparation she learns as much about who she will be talking to as she can, inevitably there are times when we all have to call an audible and make quick decisions based on the information at hand. Her focus on being present has made her more adept at this. She said she can tell when someone comes into a meeting whether they're genuinely excited about a project. "I can see in their eyes and in their faces. I can see it in the way they take notes, how they're shifting . . . is there excitement and joy in the way they're talking about the project?" In contrast, though, she can tell if someone's primary emotions are fear and anxiety, and her strategy changes accordingly. "If I get the joy version, we start brainstorming. . . . What is often negotiated out of that are things that were never on the table whatsoever. They haven't even thought of that, and I can tell they're game for it so I throw that at them. When I get the anxious person, I actually try to do less. I'll say, 'You know, I hear that you're overwhelmed by all of this. What if we break it down into these pieces?' I can see when they start to relax a little. The ultimate goal in this conversation is to get to a negotiated agreement on what work we're going to do and at what price."

The illusion of transparency

My friend Samantha worked for a company that was hiring a new manager. Part of the protocol for the interviews was that a team of six employees would sit with the candidate and ask questions, then confer afterward. When Samantha and her colleagues convened to debrief after one such interview, everyone asked Samantha why she disliked the candidate so much.

"What are you talking about?" she said. "I thought he was fine."

"Then why were you glaring at him?"

"What?" Samantha said. "I wasn't glaring."

Her colleagues assured her that yes, she was glaring. They even mimicked her expression. Samantha was horrified.

"I looked like *that*?" she asked. "I was just focusing. That was my listening face."

As Samantha now saw, her listening face looked much more like a scowl. As leadership author and speaker Carol Kinsey Goman said, "Body language is in the eye of the beholder. It has less to do with your intention and everything to do with its interpretation." Samantha was caught in what's called the *illusion of transparency*: the belief that what someone feels, desires, and intends is crystal clear to others, even though they have done very little to communicate it. There is reality, and then there is perception, and the two are not the same.

Some are uncommonly skilled at communicating just what they want to, but for most of us, getting better at it is a lifelong process. There are a few tricks to it, and none are easy.

The first is to be present. You have to be completely aware of your own emotions. You have to be aware of your facial expressions. You have to be aware not just of your words but of the tenor of the other person's words, the slight changes on their face, so that you know how they are receiving your message.

We can also ask for feedback. Samantha's colleagues teased her about her scowl-face, but she could have asked them for feedback before they had to—and the next time, she did. As soon as she left the next interview she said, "Hey, I was trying to communicate that this is an intense job but without seeming like I'm scary. Do you think I accomplished it? Do you think so-and-so actually understood what I was saying? I want to be better at this. What do you think I might do better next time?" This feedback was relevant for interviews but also for more quotidian meetings she had with her colleagues.

Samantha had a lot of work to do on her communication. If she made a scowl-face when she was in an inconsequential interview, her intensity was much more pronounced when she was in meetings where she really didn't like someone she was meeting with, or when she felt impatient because the meeting was going on for too long. She was known to tap her pencil on the desk quickly when she felt that someone was speaking unnecessarily, or when she felt the meeting should be over. She was commonly criticized for it and felt frustrated and misunderstood. When a consultant came in to help the entire team with communication, he helped Samantha practice body language that was relaxed, that signaled openness, and that employed even and deep breathing. The consultant had her focus on the speed and volume of her voice and the reception she was getting with others. Samantha began to ask specifically and deliberately for feedback.

This kind of nonverbal communication is practiced all the time in the grand national negotiation of politics. In her memoir *Becoming*, Michelle Obama writes about being called to meet with David Axelrod and Valerie Jarrett during Barack Obama's first campaign for the presidency. Michelle had been taking a lot of heat from the opposition, who tried to paint Michelle as an angry anarchist. It seemed to be working, and Michelle didn't get it. She'd been giving the same talk for months and it had seemed to resonate with her crowds. She was bringing authentic emotion and heart into her talk, she felt, but she wasn't *angry*. Then Axelrod and Jarrett muted the volume of the recording so they could examine her body language, her facial expressions. "What did I see?" she wrote. "I saw myself speaking with intensity and conviction and never letting up. I always address the tough times many Americans were facing as well as the inequities within our schools and our healthcare system. My face reflected the seriousness of what I believed was at stake, how important the choice that lay before our nation really was. But it was too serious. Too severe, at least given what people were conditioned to expect from a woman. I saw my expression as a stranger might perceive it, especially if it was framed with an unflattering message."

A consultant who joined the team advised Michelle Obama to "play to my strengths, and the things I most loved talking about, which was my love for my husband and kids, my connection to working mothers, and my proud Chicago roots," she said. The consultant recognized, too, that Michelle liked to joke around and insisted that was fine. "It was okay, in other words, to be myself."

Passion is powerful. To show others what drives you and motivates you can be very persuasive if it's well placed in a speech or a negotiation. Passion can be contagious, but it can also be misconstrued. If not well communicated, it can appear overbearing, aggressive, and unreasonable. This doesn't mean that women don't have the right to act angry; of course they do, and in other speeches when Michelle Obama wanted to convey her anger, she did. Rather, we all just need to understand how others perceive our communication, and think hard about whether the audience is getting the message intended. Striking the right balance is an art. I'm typically in favor of showing emotion in a negotiation, especially since I value human connections and honest exchange of information. But channeling our emotions effectively can be the difference between success and failure in communicating your ideas. Perception is everything and you have to understand how your words and expressions are received in order to be able to connect, deliver, influence, and impress.

Sometimes being a better communicator has nothing to do with others and everything to do with self-reflection. Self-reflection is not about judgment or about beating yourself up over communications that have gone wrong. It's about understanding. It's about taking that curiosity-driven approach you've taken to understanding others and turning it inward, so that you can learn more about yourself. It's about probing how you feel in the presence of others, and what they are doing that's making you feel that way. For instance, when I spend time with friends who are on their phone when we're together, I've gotten in the habit of doing an internal check of how I feel—which is usually tense and annoyed. I'm able to recall those feelings when I'm in conversation with others, so I'm better able to resist distractions that might have been hard for me otherwise. It's easier for me to stop my urge to reach for my phone, and to say, "Not right now."

Listening with focus

There's a popular puzzle among the elementary school set that goes something like this: Someone is found murdered on a school campus at the beginning of the school year. The PE teacher said she couldn't have been the killer because she was watching students run laps. The principal says it wasn't her because she was giving a tour of the school. The math teacher says it wasn't him because he was grading midterms. Who's lying?

The answer is the math teacher, because he said he was grading midterms, and yet the murder happened at the beginning of the year. The puzzle tests your listening skills to see what information you're discarding too readily when it's actually important. Likewise, a critical piece of any negotiation is to focus on taking in information, and then thoughtfully and methodically analyzing it. You cannot discard any piece of information as unimportant. Everything is important, until it's not.

Listening well is also strategic because when your counterpart feels like they are your focus, they are more likely to open up. You gather more information, and you can better understand the other side's perspective so that you know better how to frame your argument.

With mindful listening, you focus on listening to *everything*. It sounds so simple, right? But my students report that the mindful listening activity is the hardest part of my class. In an exercise I highly recommend you replicate, I ask them to find a partner and sit across from them. It's important with mindful listening that both people are at the same level, so they are seeing eye to eye. Then one person speaks for five minutes about whatever it is they want. It could be something that happened that day. It could be what they're thinking of making for dinner that night. It could be a meaningful, powerful memory they want to share. The listener has to focus on what his partner is saying, and not on what to say in response, or what to say when they swap roles and it's his turn to speak for three minutes. The listener can ask clarifying or follow-up questions but needs to be careful not to judge—which even includes making affirmative declarations like, "Wow, that must have been hard," or "Yum, that sounds delicious." Mindful listening is just taking in. It takes focus, concentration, and patience.

In a negotiation, you probably won't use mindful listening but rather active listening where you *do* make affirmative declarations. Yet I still recommend practicing mindful listening, because it strengthens those muscles of focus. It's like lifting weights to help you prepare to run a marathon—every good trainer will tell you that cross-training is essential. There's much more to listening than we give it credit for, and you have to work hard to control your thoughts and otherwise build the skills required to be good at it. If, when your negotiation partner is speaking to you, you're focused on what you'll say in response, you are in danger of missing a key piece of information from them. As Stephen Covey famously put it in his seminal book *The 7 Habits of Highly Effective People*, "Most people do not listen with the intent to understand; they listen with the intent to reply." Perhaps you're worried, though—you don't want to have your counterpart turn to you when they're done speaking and say, "Well?" and feel like you've been so focused on listening that you haven't thought of a response. You don't want the scary silence that follows (see Chapter 2!). Remind yourself it's okay. Give yourself permission to take information in before thinking about how to respond to it. Don't let feeling rushed cloud your judgment. It's fine to say, "Let me think about this for a few minutes."

One of the more natural results of teaching listening skills is that I've become more aware of my own. And I've noticed that improving my listening has deepened my relationships. I make connections with people more quickly than I used to, which is saying something because I'm an introvert. It appears subtle, but I see the difference. For instance, I have a friend who recently lost her high-level job. Though she had seen the writing on the wall and knew it was coming, she'd received the news much earlier than she expected. We met for drinks, and it was clear she was still reeling from it. My first instinct was to tell her about the experience of losing my job that I recounted in Chapter 2. I had never told her that story before and thought it would be helpful because it would show her how much I understood. But I stopped myself. I needed to hear her—really hear her—before saying anything. There were key differences in our experiences—mine had happened early in my career, whereas she was deeply into hers. It wouldn't work to say, "I know exactly how you feel because I was there." Well, that's not true. I didn't know how she felt, not really, unless I listened. My experience might not resonate. I needed to listen purely, without thought to what I would say.

Managing emotions

Part of what makes active listening so difficult in negotiation is that people are often anxious about the negotiation to begin with. If you're infected by fear, if you're activating your amygdala, the "fight-or-flight" part of your brain, listening well and focusing are virtually impossible. Now, a little bit of anxiety—or rather worry—will make you more motivated for a negotiation, more prepared, and will keep your senses sharp during the negotiation. But too much fear and worry and you can't think straight. You have to adjust so that you're in the sweet spot—you have to be a master of managing emotions.

There is a famous quote from psychiatrist Viktor Frankl: "Between stimulus and response there is space. In that space is the power to choose our response. In our response lies our growth and our freedom." The quote is like a battle cry for mindfulness. Mindfulness has long left the realm of yogis and philosophers and permeated the rest of the world. It doesn't matter whether you're at the bargaining table or the Thanksgiving dinner table; mindfulness helps you acknowledge and regulate your emotions.

The best course of action you can take to manage your emotions during a negotiation is to think through them fully *before* a negotiation. Most people have had the experience of waking up in the middle of the night, or perhaps not being able to sleep to begin with, because they are in the throes of a heated argument with someone . . . all in their head. Fuming and ruminating are a preparation, of sorts—they signal to you that when you do eventually talk with the other person, you will be bringing some strong feelings into the discussion. Thus, you need to figure out what those strong feelings are, where they're coming from, and how you can best use them to serve the negotiation. Note that I'm not telling you not to be yourself. Be yourself, just be the best-prepared, most emotionally attuned version of yourself you can be.

If the primary feeling you're bringing into the discussion is anger, beware. Whereas once it was commonly accepted that anger was a useful emotion in a negotiation, that's not so. Researchers in a seminal 1997 study found that angry negotiators and their counterparts had less desire to work with each other in the future, they achieved fewer joint gains, and the party who was angry did not in fact claim any more value for themselves by virtue of being angry. More recent research shows that when people are faced with an angry negotiator, they're more likely to walk away.

Anne was in the difficult spot of leading a board wherein one member, Melissa, was often divisive and abrasive. Melissa would frequently begin her emails by attacking someone's intentions, and, as the board members were all volunteers who gave their time out of goodwill, Anne was protective of her colleagues and frequently furious with Melissa. She could feel her blood pressure rise whenever she saw Melissa's name in her in-box. After a particularly nasty email fight between Melissa and some of the other board members, Anne decided to take Melissa out for coffee. She really didn't want to but felt she might be able to appeal to her in a way that would help the group's dynamic going forward.

Before their meeting, Anne thought through all the ways that Melissa might push her buttons and incite her anger. It had happened before at board meetings, many times. Anne's de facto response was to shut her down, to take control of the conversation and steer it away from Melissa. Anne had a temper, and not a lot of patience for bullshit when there was a lot of important work to be done. In sum, Anne knew this coffee date had the potential to go very, very badly. But the whole objective was to work toward a better, more collaborative relationship, so Anne couldn't let the discussion go off the rails. She planned what she would do if Melissa attacked— how she would breathe and touch the table to calm herself, how she would leave a pause before she responded, how she would check the timbre of her voice when she spoke. She thought through how she would absolutely not drink coffee at their meeting, which made her jumpy and sped up her voice, and instead would order herbal tea. If she was really becoming angry, she would imagine that she was taking part in a story told by her favorite satirist, David Sedaris. By focusing on Melissa's absurdity, she could laugh inwardly and do what she had to do outwardly.

Although sometimes the best course for dealing with a difficult person is to keep the meeting as focused and businesslike as possible, Anne sensed that with Melissa, it was all *about* the small talk—the whole point was to let go of an agenda and let her talk. And indeed, the more rapport you have with your counterpart before and during a negotiation, the more you can keep anger at bay. Anne suspected Melissa needed an audience to say all that she wanted to say without rebuttal. After a half hour of talking, wherein Anne asked friendly questions that she knew would put Melissa at ease and make her feel comfortable, they delved into some of the more loaded issues that had come up with the board. Anne let Melissa talk—and she could talk *a lot*. Anne reminded herself to stay present, that she didn't need to cut Melissa off as she often had to during board meetings. She could just listen and watch. What she saw was a great deal of hurt and vulnerability. Melissa didn't outright say, "I'm hurt and vulnerable," of course, but there were clear clues. In an offhand way, Melissa offered that she had not attended their last board meeting because she thought everyone hated her. She told the story of how one board member had given her a hug when they'd seen each other randomly. It was clear from her body language when she told the story that the interaction had mattered to her, a lot. Anne learned more by being present at that coffee date than she had in a year of working on the board with Melissa. Seeing Melissa's insecurity taught Anne that Melissa needed reassurance, to feel safe. And if Melissa felt safe, her actual point of view came through instead of getting lost in divisive language.

It was worth Anne's time to engage Melissa because it had the potential to save tons of time at board meetings, so the group could more effectively focus on the agenda at hand. And it did work, for about one meeting. Then Melissa returned to her divisive tactics.

Anne could have mentally prepared herself to negotiate with her one-on-one again, but she determined it just wasn't worth it and that the board needed to seek another way to proceed. (One that involved squeezing Melissa out, unfortunately.) There comes a point in many negotiations where you have to make a call about whether it makes sense to engage at all. (This is a particularly important internal check to do before talking to intractable family members about politics.) In short, just because you're capable of managing your emotions, it doesn't mean you always want to. Sometimes, simply walking away from difficult negotiation partners is the smartest thing to do.

Many negotiators go a step beyond managing their emotions for a particular encounter and work to make mindfulness more instinctive by practicing meditation; Ford Motor's Bill Ford, Salesforce's Marc Benioff, Amy Schumer, and Arianna Huffington are among those who are committed meditators. Others practice yoga, like my student Julia. "Yoga offers some of the few moments in my everyday life where I unplug," she said. "At my studio, we literally leave our phones in the other room." Her yoga practice of focusing on the world of her mat helps her manage the times when she's distracted at her consulting job. "Sometimes I realize I have a ticker tape going full of the stories I tell myself about what other people think of me. It's really demotivating, distracting, and unproductive, which is why the focus I am able to cultivate on the yoga mat is so valuable." Finding ways to quiet her mind is important to her in general, but it also translates directly to who she is as a negotiator. When you're in the middle of a challenging conversation, she said, "you don't want to be thinking about the eight other things you have to do for work. Or thinking, 'Oh, I said this thing and I shouldn't have and now they probably think I'm an idiot.'"

Despite her regular practice, Julia still struggles with noticing her internal monologue and watching it, as if it's floating by on a cloud or on a river, but without being swept up in it. It's a form of detachment, what William Ury has termed "going to the balcony." You want to see what's happening, and acknowledge what you're thinking and feeling but with a little remove. You want to think, *Hmm . . . I am having some strong thoughts and feelings right now*, but not act on them without giving yourself that blessed space that Frankl wrote about.

"Last week at work I had a client say something to me that took me off guard," Julia said. "The client was surprised at a decision one of their counterparts had made to extend the scope of our contract beyond the original end date. . . . We were going to be helping them with another module of work. I sensed a reaction that wasn't pleasure, excitement, or gratitude at first blush. So it had to do with me, but it didn't have to do with me. But the way it was phrased, it felt personal.

"My initial reaction was 'Shit, this is bad, this is really bad. They don't want our help, we're not demonstrating enough value.' My brain starts going. In that moment, the story mill started," she said. She worried about what the client had said or thought about her, and what she might have done wrong. "Anything I could dream up was running through my head," she said. "In those moments, it's very hard to remember that I'm drawing conclusions about what's happening around me that may not be helpful or true."

She called forth her practice and noted that when you're successfully mindful, you recognize the thoughts, observe them, honor them, then let them go. "I thought, *Hmm, I see that thought. I'm going to allow it to float away in the sky. I'm going to focus on the present moment, what is real right now and not a concern that I'm fabricating in my head*. Because the stories you tell yourself don't help," she added. "Unless the story is 'You're amazing!,' it's usually negative and brings you down."

Although Julia's remedy is yoga, you have to do what works for you, with the ultimate goal of noticing that inner critic and getting some distance. I struggle with doubts and negative self-talk all the time, and I turn to the polar opposite of what works for Julia: I go to SoulCycle. That place is a respite for me—there are no phones, it's a dark room lit only by the glow of candles, and music plays so loudly that you can't hear yourself think. All you can focus on is the intensity of the required effort as sweat drips down your face, your breathlessness while enjoying the endorphin high. At the end of the class, having had a complete vacation from my thoughts, I'm almost always able to think with more objectivity.

There are many ways to think about and practice presence, whether you're leaving your phone before going to a party, staring at the sunset from an airplane window, or practicing yoga. But one of my favorite ways to frame presence comes from my student Glen. Glen has been playing the guitar since he was five and likens the notion of presence to that of differentiating musical notes. "I think the most incredible thing that I was able to achieve at a certain point," he said of his music, "was not to play more notes or to play faster but to leave more space between the notes. What makes music music is leaving space," he said. Otherwise, the notes just blend together and that's not music—it's noise. Ever since he shared this with me, I've thought of presence as the space between the notes. It could be infinitesimal. It could be subtle. But without it, it's all just noise.

CHAPTER 8

assume abundance

On a Monday last winter, I reported for jury duty in D.C., where I live, and after waiting around all morning I was one of the potential jurors selected for a panel. The judge gave us the rough outline of the case we'd be hearing—which seemed very simple and sure to wrap up that day. Then he asked us to come to the lectern to see him if there was any possibility we wouldn't be able to serve for four consecutive days. *Dammit*, I thought. I had to teach a class in New York on Wednesday morning that I could not miss. Despite the judge's question, I knew the case couldn't last very long, so if I just stayed quiet I'd be able to finish out my service by the end of the day or the following day. Additionally, since the final jury panel hadn't been selected, I could actually be dismissed, which would fulfill my jury duty obligations. But I was in a court of law and didn't feel I could withhold information when the judge requested us to be forthcoming.

I told the judge about my conflict, so he excused me from the panel and sent me to the schedulers. What followed felt straight out of a *Seinfeld* episode. The clerk I approached looked grumpy and harassed the moment she turned her attention to me. When I explained the situation, she said I could leave but would need to choose another Monday within ninety days to report back.

"That's going to be a problem," I explained, "because starting next week I teach every Tuesday in Philadelphia and I won't be able to stay past Mondays. We'd naturally run into the same issue next time around and even worse, since I'd only have the Monday to spare at that point."

She shrugged impassively. "You'll still need to choose a date."

"But then I'll spend my whole morning waiting around for the same exact thing to happen, and I'll be standing in front of you again saying the exact same thing. Can't I be called in for trials that take place on Wednesdays instead?"

"No," she said. "If you're initially called for a Monday appearance, you *have* to choose another Monday."

"Well, then can I come in on a Monday in May, when the semester's over and I won't have to teach?"

"No," she said. "That's outside of the ninety days." She then went on to lecture me about my duty as a citizen.

The most frustrating part of this experience was that I *wanted* to do my duty as a citizen. I even wanted to serve on a jury. I thought it would actually be an interesting process—especially from a perspective of negotiation. I wasn't making up excuses to get out of it. I'm sure this clerk was so accustomed to being lied to that she couldn't see that my intentions were good. I'm also sure that there are valid reasons for the many rules regarding a juror's service, but she never explained them, so I couldn't rationalize them. But I was trying to present my intent, and I was trying to figure out a way that I could serve and also teach my class. All of my ideas fell on deaf ears, or, rather, prompted lectures about citizenship responsibilities.

The scheduler's inflexibility reminded me of what my students do in class. They become singularly focused on one thing and one thing only: what slice of the pie they can grab for themselves in a negotiation. It's like they're wearing dog cones, unable to see beyond what's immediately in front of them (dog food!). The problem-solving part of their brain isn't available to them because they're entirely focused on fighting for their share.

We wear dog cones all the time and we don't even realize it. And the reason we do so is the same as this scheduler's: We are in a locked mind-set, a state in which *no* is just so easy to say. And it is often much easier to see only our narrow piece than it is to see our negotiating partner as someone who might have overlapping interests. We enter every negotiation fearful that the other person is out to get us, that we must be cutthroat and competitive instead of kind, honest, and open. I'm sure the scheduler had heard a million excuses. I'm certain her nerves had already been worked by the time I arrived at the counter. I'm sure she had a variety of great reasons for her inflexibility. But it was maddening that there was no room for compromise.

No matter the circumstance, in order to get to yes and beyond, we need to be thoughtful about the ways we limit our thinking, and why, and think more expansively about what's possible. As Winston Churchill said, "The pessimist sees difficulty in every opportunity. The optimist sees opportunity in every difficulty."

In this chapter, you'll see how assuming that there's enough for everyone—abundance—can lead to uncovering overlapping interests, create more options for problem solving, and allow you more leverage by giving you the courage to walk away. Most significantly, when we start from a place of abundance and not scarcity, instead of splitting up our pie, we make a bigger one.

When you're *sure* there's not enough

I have seen "scarcity thinking" in classrooms, jury rooms, airport lines, and especially the workplace. For instance, I have worked in the sports industry in many different capacities for almost fifteen years, and although I've seen growing gender diversity, it continues to be male-dominated. The scarcity of female executives can breed competition, just as it does with other male-dominated industries like technology, finance, and law. Studies show that women would prefer to work for men than for other women, and in a study comparing attitudes at law firms, the firms where women were less represented, the women who did work there were "almost universally reviled" by the other women. Women are sadly so much tougher on one another professionally, aggressively jostling to maintain their position at the leadership level. They see it as a battle to succeed in a hypercompetitive environment, where they perceive there are few token females allowed and they need to be one of them. Work collaboratively with another woman when there may be only room for one of us? No way.

The reality is, we're all pretty conditioned to think there's limited room at the top, and just one way to get there. One student, Heather, did better than anyone else in her class on the exercise where she had to sell a tonic, and when I pointed out that she hadn't been able to justify her outsized ask, it rattled her. "But I got the best deal of anyone in the class." Although it's true that she had done well, it was also true that she'd gotten lucky. Heather's negotiation partner hadn't questioned why she was asking so much for the tonic. And luck does not make for a sustainable strategy. It's also likely that her classmates would remember her unjustifiable ask. In the real world, she'd gain a reputation as someone who was unreasonable or greedy. In class, she would put her peers on guard.

When you look at a negotiation as winner-take-all, you lose out on creative thinking and options that neither party might have considered on their own. You're unable to see beyond the competition, like the remorseful Aaron Burr from Lin-Manuel Miranda's *Hamilton*: "I should've known the world was wide enough for both Hamilton and me."

My student Eszter was brought up in Communist Hungary, not exactly an ideal environment for nurturing an abundance mindset, since every resource imaginable was distributed in a careful and restricted way. Her grandfather was jailed for criticizing the government; the family sought refugee status in Canada but was ultimately rejected. After the Berlin Wall fell, they had to return to Hungary. "I know from my grandma that things were hard when I was small," Eszter said. "We didn't have money for bread and could only heat one part of our apartment." Although Eszter's mom was a doctor and her father was a lawyer, the family earned the same amount as every other family. "In a capitalistic society you have opportunities to think outside the box," Eszter explained. "But with communism the box is by definition quite limited—you can only get a passport every few years, you don't get to buy things because you only have a designated amount of money, you can't get currency. . . . My mom was the mastermind of trying to make something more out of it. How do you take what seems like the same as everyone else and try to transform it into something more?" Eszter says that because of the way her mother operated, she had a great childhood and always considered herself privileged. Her mother's creative think-ing created abundance where there didn't seem to be any. "We didn't buy ice cream," Eszter says, "but [my mom] told us that because we are so good at saving on ice cream, we would be able to have choco-late cake later. I think in the end it was the thought and anticipation of the chocolate cake that made us feel that there was abundance. It was in the reframing. We weren't a family unable to afford ice cream, we were a family making a conscious choice to save wisely for the future.

"When we had enough money for chocolate cake, she said we could have the chocolate cake *or* we could now buy ice cream and save for something even better than a chocolate cake."

In this way, Eszter learned how to make more from what you've got. When she was just seven, she went on an errand to get napkins. Eszter's mom had given her the precise amount of money needed for two packs of napkins. "I remember bartering my way through the market, asking who would give me a better price or better deal, or something as a gift for the purchase." The final merchant she spoke with asked Eszter why she was working so hard to get a deal. "I told her that I needed enough money left over to buy flowers for my mom as a surprise. I told her something like 'There is no deal without it.'" The merchant was not swayed by Eszter's threat, obviously, but im-pressed by her precociousness and intent to please. When Eszter came home, she had not only the napkins but also flowers for her mom.

When Eszter graduated from Penn she worked as a strategy consultant and (because why not do *more*?) she also started an on-line retailer with her boyfriend, who would become her husband. Their venture was successful and so they started several more, ulti-mately selling them all in order to focus on a new consulting business they formed together. Eszter negotiates all the time in her work and always tries to view the negotiation as a collaborative, rather than competitive, venture. One of Eszter's trademark moves after getting to a good deal is to turn to her negotiation partner and say, "Great, we have a good deal. Now, can we make it better?" I recommend this tactic all the time, and although most people agree with it, few actually do it. But Eszter does. It may look like taking a few minutes to go over all of the new information the negotiating partners have learned about one another. Is there another area where they should engage in business together? Anything else they can do, maybe as part of the original deal or maybe outside it, that would be mutually beneficial? Eszter consistently analyzes whether she's approaching a deal differently based on whether there will be a next one, and she says it's her moral obligation to treat every deal as if there *will* be. And, in fact, she has been surprised by the people who have returned to her orbit when she never expected them to.

In one personal investment deal, Eszter negotiated with a large real estate development company—let's call them ARCO—about the purchase of a flat in Budapest. The deal was pretty complicated, but what it boiled down to was that the property—which was still under construction—was smaller than ARCO would admit. "I knew they were wrong, so I asked for their calculations." She went over everything with a fine-tooth comb and could show that she was right. Still, no law firm would agree to represent her. "They said it's impossible to go up against this company, even though they knew I was probably right."

So Eszter wrote ARCO a letter instead. She indicated that although the company might not have meant it, its information about the size of the flat was incorrect. She explained that their dispute could be reduced to mathematics, that in this case there was no he said/she said. She said that she would not sign a contract unless an independent third party verified the measurements. ARCO did not respond kindly and went with the strongman approach instead, getting as many as six of its lawyers involved. "They told me we would be in litigation for five years if I didn't sign. But I wouldn't. Then [ARCO] said, 'You have no rights and you have no power. You're not going to get anywhere. You have to sign this or you lose.'"

Most people, when faced with such a predicament, would either sign or steel themselves for litigation. And in this case, surely ARCO hadn't given Eszter any reason to work together or to believe any form of collaboration was possible. It was trying to bully her into compliance. "So I told myself to isolate the negative parts of the negotiation," she said. When she did, possibilities opened up. Eszter did two things to push once more for a collaborative—versus a strictly competitive—process: First, she reached out to the construction lead on the site. "I talked to everyone kindly and asked about the challenges with the project. I do this normally—I wasn't on a spy mission to collect information. Being on good terms with the site lead and project engineers allowed me to understand the motivations of certain behaviors during the later negotiations with the lawyers."

Second, she wrote another letter to ARCO. She said she understood that their last encounter had been negative, and that she wanted to change the focus to something more positive. She gave them three different options that she felt comfortable with, including one that involved Eszter buying something else from them. If they agreed to one, she said, they would have a deal.

Significantly, Eszter had learned from the site engineers that the reason the flat was smaller than promised was due to a construction issue and that all of the flats on that side of the building were smaller. She could easily have included this information in the letter and threatened that if ARCO did not work with her, she would go to the other flat owners and begin a collective campaign to sue. In fact, she actually *did* include a subtle reference to this information in her first draft but then took it out, reasoning that she couldn't very well present a positive framing of the deal if she was also threatening ARCO. "If I couldn't 'win' this without the threat, then I wouldn't feel good about it. That's the way I now think about negotiations. If you can't do it the right way, the result is not valuable." The intent of interest-based negotiation, after all, is "to bring people to their senses rather than to their knees." Interest-based negotiation is about problem solving, not winning. It's about seeing the interests of both parties and figuring out a way to meet them in a way that everyone feels comfortable. Winning takes on a different meaning. It's not about one-way gains but about shared gains that can set the stage for future opportunities.

ARCO ended up selecting one of the three options Eszter had proposed, and they made a deal. What's more, when ARCO had an issue come up with another project soon after, they asked Eszter to be a consultant on it because they trusted her.

Perhaps my favorite story of Eszter's abundance mind-set doesn't have to do with business at all. She and her husband and brother wanted to take her dad to his favorite restaurant for his birthday, but somehow they had botched the reservation. The maître d' was kind but firm that there was no table.

"I smiled and walked away," said Eszter, "but then came back to him with a couple of ideas of what we could do. I suggested that they add a table for us in the sun, which we don't mind (they had a limited number of covered areas, but I saw more tables/chairs in the storage area when I walked around); or that we wait for the fifteen-minute mark (how long they hold no-show reservations) on tables that were reserved."

The maître d' said no, he was sorry, but there was simply no room for them that evening. Eszter walked away again and thought for a moment. Then she went back to the maître d' and explained that as the evening was so lovely and the part of town the restaurant was in was so charming, they would take a short walk, and then she would come back to see if either she or the maître d' had thought of a solution that might work. "I thought that even if there was not a no-show, this would give the staff time to think of a solution without pressure. Sometimes I find that people think of a solution just after one's walked away—I know this, because sometimes I go back."

Sure enough, when she and her family returned fifteen minutes later, the maître d' said he now had a table. Would she like it?

Note that Eszter wasn't obnoxious to the guy. This wasn't about refusing to hear no, or simply repeating "But I really want a table" again and again. Rather, she was thinking about the lack of a table as a problem to be solved, and one that she and the maître d' could work on collaboratively. She didn't have a "locked" mind-set, one where she might have shrugged in defeat in the face of a seemingly intractable problem. She chose to see the situation differently.

"After we had a lovely lunch, I went up to personally thank everyone involved in making the table happen and explained how much it meant to my dad to have lunch with his kids (who live abroad) on his birthday. They all felt like heroes by the end," she said. "We tipped well, but I specifically did not want to give them a tip for the table, because I wanted the interaction to be based on kindness between humans and not based on a monetary transaction."

It's so tempting to fall into a locked mind-set because it's often easier to categorize a problem as impossible to solve, to say "no" and "can't" than to try to creatively work together. When working with someone with such a mind-set, sometimes it takes several tries to shift them into a problem-solving frame of mind. Recently I went to a department store to return two dresses I'd bought that, once I got them home, I realized didn't fit me all that well. I'd lost my receipt, but the tags were still on the dresses, so I wasn't anticipating a problem. I explained the receipt issue to the salesclerk. "Can you look it up through my credit card?" I asked, knowing they often have transaction histories that will show how much someone has paid for the item.

"No," she said, "I can't, because you bought it from the couture collection. For those areas we need a receipt."

I believed her; I understood that this was their policy. But why? The policy itself made no sense to me, so I asked her to explain. "You pay more so you need a receipt?" I asked.

She shrugged. "On the tag," she said, pointing to a tag on one of the dresses, "it says that you need your receipt for these items."

She was right, of course, it did. I said I understood it was the policy (although come on, who *really* reads the print on a tag?), but the why didn't make sense to me. "So what can I do here?" I asked her, hoping she'd help me problem-solve.

She said she was sorry—and I know she really was—but that she couldn't let me return it without a receipt.

At that point I was considering my remaining option, which was to give the dresses away. Why not just offer them to her?

"Would these fit you?" I asked. "Because if not, I'm donating them to Goodwill. Consider it a gift from me to you." I was being serious. Absurd but serious.

She raised her eyebrows, then peered at me closely. "I'll tell you what," she said. "We can find the transaction if you remember which register they were purchased on. So maybe, if you could remember which register rung up the purchase . . ."

"I can!" I said, and pointed to what turned out to be Register 5. It took forty-five minutes, all told, from the moment I walked in until she found the receipt. By the end of the time we were really friendly, in the hunt together. Instead of just giving me store credit for the dresses, which was their policy, she ended up refunding the money to my credit card.

Naturally, this pressing to problem-solving mode doesn't work all the time. It certainly didn't work with the jury duty clerk. But it's worth trying to (nicely) help someone enter that frame of mind.

What dog cones have to do with ethics

People tend to see two ways of negotiating: a cutthroat style that assumes there's not enough to go around, and an abundance style that assumes there is. What so often happens when we take the latter approach, one based in problem-solving and a clear desire to find mutual gains, is that we're labeled inexperienced or naïve. And what so often happens when we take the cutthroat approach is that we're labeled competitive and uncompromising. In this section, I get into why the *naïve* label is misguided, while the other one . . . well, it's up for debate.

Stacey started a social mission–driven company in Detroit that does custom screen printing and serves as a community gathering place. Her community-mindedness made her nervous to take a negotiations course when she was enrolled in the Goldman Sachs 10,000 Small Businesses program. "Negotiations sounds so intimidating," she said. "I always thought of negotiators as people who were good wheelers and dealers. People who got the upper hand and kept it."

She was encouraged, then, by my discussions in class about how negotiation is best seen as a conversation, one in which strong relationships are key. She was skilled at building relationships and loved to learn about people, so she thought perhaps the class would resonate with her after all.

I broke Stacey's class into groups to do an exercise in which four different companies try to buy the same object from one seller. The stakes were high: Each party, including the seller, could lose their job if not successful. Although many of the exercises I use in class don't have a clear wrong or right answer, this particular exercise does. There is a solution for all parties, where everyone can get what they want if they lay their cards on the table. I love showing the various outcomes to the class when we debrief, because it provides the most remarkable "aha" moments. *If only we'd been more open about what we were after*, they see, *we'd have all come away happy.* Although egos are sometimes hurt and students become defensive, this reaction is often followed by an awareness that win-win solutions are in fact possible, and that the path to getting there requires curiosity, an open exchange of information, honesty, and respect.

Stacey didn't know any of this, of course, when she went into the exercise. But she approached the negotiation as a conversation, asking questions about her negotiating partners' interests and revealing her own. "The people in my group were looking to win," she said. "That was hard for me. And they were looking at me as naïve because I wasn't interested in holding my cards close." In this exercise, much like all of the other negotiation role-plays, participants react as they would in real life. If they perceive scarcity, their dog cones come out and block open and innovative problem solving. As a result, they can't find a path to collaborative outcomes.

By the end of the exercise, Stacey's group was close to coming to blows and failed to reach their optimal solution. Stacey also didn't come out of the negotiation as well as some of her counterparts.

When we debriefed as a class, Stacey realized that two of her negotiation partners had misled her about what they needed and what
they had to spend. They were operating from a cutthroat perspective. "I felt really used and betrayed," she remembered. "I thought
we were negotiating in good faith. I felt like I'd been had." She asked
me in front of the whole class, "What do you do when the people
you're negotiating with don't negotiate in an ethical way?" I could
hear murmurs throughout the room as people realized that we were
heading into a difficult conversation. Her classmates had not seen
Stacey like this before, but she was angry and hurt.

"Did you get at least the minimum you were supposed to get for
your company?" I asked.

"Yes," Stacey said.

"Did you feel good about the way you personally acted, that you
acted with integrity? Did you stay true to yourself?"

"Yes."

"Then you made a good deal." I wanted to impress on her the
advice that's been handed down for centuries and yet is so hard
to internalize: Ultimately, we can only affect what's within our
control. Stacey would be more effective—not to mention more
content—if she kept her focus on her actions.

The class grew heated, with some people saying they had similar experiences to Stacey's, and criticizing their classmates for their
misleading behavior. Other students insisted that their "winner-
take-all" approach was the only sensible way. Sure, they argued, in
this case there was an outcome that worked for everyone, but their
objective was to find and hold on to their leverage at all costs.

Stacey went home that night still feeling lousy about what had
happened. "Then later on," she said, "I was unpacking it in my mind
and I started feeling better. I shifted away from thinking *Maybe I*

should have tried to get a better deal to No, I wouldn't feel good about screwing someone."

When Stacey talked to her group in a later session, one classmate condescendingly reflected on Stacy's approach, telling her, "You seemed so naïve. I wanted to help you out." Stacey was understandably frustrated that her approach was seen as amateurish instead of principled. So she told her group "I'm not being naïve, I just don't want to play a game if I don't have to. It doesn't feel good. Even if I were to win, it still wouldn't feel good."

Over the long run, an open negotiation style can be rewarding. The reality is that, if you can help it, you're only going to negotiate once with a person who tries to screw you. And in fact, one of the women from Stacey's group later needed to have some T-shirts printed and negotiated with Stacey using similar sharp-elbowed tactics that she had used in class. This women made a very big deal about the fact that she was also considering using another classmate's company for the order. This woman loved to create competition where there was none, a phenomenon I see frequently but that always baffles me. Stacey did the work for her but found the process just as unpleasant as their negotiation in class. So Stacey resolved that she would never work with her again. In contrast, Stacey formed a friendship with another woman in her group who shared Stacey's point of view that it was senseless to play games if you didn't have to. They bonded over their shared values and remain close professional supporters.

The fundamental argument in Stacey's group is one I see a lot, as negotiators constantly wrestle with establishing the line between being a savvy negotiator and an unethical counterparty. Not everyone who follows the school of the cutthroat negotiator is unethical, but it can be a slippery slope. There's a process researchers have described as "ethical fading," wherein "the ethical colors of a moral decision fade into bleached hues . . . void of moral implications." At the heart of this is self-deception, or, essentially, the way we lie to ourselves about our behavior so we can still sleep at night.

Many people are comfortable with whatever approach achieves their desired outcome. "Who cares if I'm perceived as less than forthright?" they may think. "I got the outcome I wanted, and I'm never going to see this person again. I won!" This was certainly the point of view of many in Stacey's group. We are programmed to think that all negotiations are competitive, so a transparent approach can only hurt you. In fact, in many negotiations classes, you're graded solely on the outcome of your negotiations. I think this view of negotiation is shortsighted. And I'm in good company.

In 1873, Andrew Carnegie had a problem. The financial market was in panic, and to honor his commitments he needed to liquidate some funds he had invested with J. P. Morgan. He asked Morgan for $60,000, as his original investment was $50,000 and he figured its value had increased $10,000. Morgan could have written him a check for $60,000 and let that be the end of it. But Morgan knew that the value had actually increased by $20,000, so he wrote a check for $70,000. Because of Morgan's integrity, Carnegie was loyal to him for the rest of his life.

A cynic might find this story quaint. *Sure, maybe reputation mattered in 1873*, they might say, *but welcome to the present, where the savvy negotiator must be cutthroat in order to win.*

I disagree, but I also believe that each individual must establish her own ethical lines. Some questions of ethics are easily answered: I could never accept, for example, lying to a counterpart about core issues. But there are a lot of gray areas, and questions about honesty come up more often than you might suspect. Some people think there is no harm in a little white lie, so they have no problem making a minor misstatement. Telling a negotiating partner that you were late because of traffic when you actually overslept doesn't affect the negotiation substance, so no harm, no foul, right? In certain cultures, deceit in a negotiation is seen as standard, so even more substantive lies are not seen as immoral. For others, there is no such thing as an acceptable mistruth—a lie is a lie is a lie.

I'm not prescriptive around what constitutes ethical negotiation, because that would imply that my judgment is correct, and that's simply not so. Rather, I work with my students to help them understand *their* values, and how to bring these convictions to their negotiations. Reaching this understanding is an ongoing and lifelong exercise for all of us.

Most critically, negotiators must determine whether their actions would violate their own moral code. As Stacey realized, a one-time favorable outcome cannot come at the cost of your principles. She had to think, if her actions were covered on the front page of the *Wall Street Journal*, would she be okay with that? Would she still feel she'd taken the right approach? More important, had she been true to herself? Would regret keep her up at night?

Even if certain negotiating tactics don't sacrifice your principles, there are important strategic reasons to consider the implications of how you negotiate. First, every negotiator should consider how their counterpart would react to any perceived dishonesty. Some people think, *It's a negotiation and I expect them to lie.* But if you're negotiating with someone who believes that even small mistruths are unforgivable, she may never work with you again if you intentionally mislead her. Some others have even less tolerance and believe that failing to disclose information is tantamount to a lie. With such a broad spectrum of beliefs, you have to make sure you understand your negotiating partner (remember Chapters 5 and 6!) and ensure that your approach is tailored appropriately.

Honesty in negotiation is also important because it helps you maintain your credibility throughout the process. The nuance of ethics comes to the forefront with a simple example of stating your final "bottom line." Let's say you're interested in buying a souvenir and, in an effort to drive down the price, you tell the seller that you just can't pay more than $10. If the vendor responds, "That's too bad, I can't sell it for that"—well, now what? Your misstatement has trapped you. You don't want to walk away—you actually want the keepsake, and the truth is, you were prepared to pay more. So you tell the vendor, "Fine. I'll give you $11.50." You've lost all credibility. The seller now knows you misstated your true bottom line and is unlikely to believe your future protestations.

Most people shrug when they hear this example, thinking it's an inconsequential negotiation. And bartering over a vacation trinket is hardly life and death. But credibility in negotiation is critical, and it can be destroyed whether or not your counterpart shares your definition of a white lie. Words matter. And if you blow your credibility on something small, you've also blown it on whatever follows. If your counterpart believes that you are not being forthright, he will be on edge and will scrutinize all future claims, if he is even willing to continue negotiating at all.

Another simply tactical reason to avoid saying anything that's not completely true is that you don't have to keep track of possible misstatements. No one wants to spend their time and energy in a negotiation keeping track of little white lies: *What was the excuse I gave for being late? What did I say my available funds were?* With the truth, you don't need to remember what you've said and to whom.

Although I avoid dictating others' ethical lines in negotiation, I have certainly developed my own views of what constitutes fair—and effective—behavior. Personally, I share the perspective of the late Jon Huntsman Sr., the self-made billionaire who cofounded and ran the massive Huntsman Corporation. "Financial ends never justify unethical means," he wrote in his book *Winners Never Cheat*. He understood that it takes years to establish a reputation and only hours to dismantle it. "Once dishonesty is introduced," he wrote, "distrust becomes the hallmark of future dealings or associations." Huntsman worked in the Nixon White House, so he saw firsthand how underhanded tactics caused leaders to lose their reputations (and ultimately their jobs). Huntsman also relates how his company's ethical stand proved time and again to be profitable over the long term. For example, Huntsman Chemical worked in partnership with Mitsubishi in Thailand, but when Jon Huntsman learned that his company was expected to pay bribes, Huntsman Corporation sold its interest at a $3 million loss. Jon Huntsman was playing the long game. "Ethical decisions can be cumbersome and unprofitable in the near term," he reflected, "but after our refusal to pay 'fees' in Thailand became known, we never had a problem over bribes again in that part of the world."

Jon Huntsman fully acknowledged—indeed, embraced—that competition is central to the entrepreneurial spirit, and negotiations are often tough. But cheating and lying are a step beyond. "If the immoral nature of cheating and lying doesn't particularly bother you," he wrote, "think about this: They eventually lead to failure."

Conversely, when you're known as someone who plays fair, who is honorable and trustworthy, you are rewarded. Every holiday, Linda Schlesinger-Wagner asks her staff at Skinnytees to make a list of their favorite customers. Not their biggest customers, but the ones that they like working with the most. Those customers get 25 percent off their next order. It's Santa saying, "I've been watching, and you're pretty good."

Honesty and respect reap rewards over and over, and when you project these qualities outward, you get returns. This isn't just a would-be episode of *SuperSoul Sunday*—though I love that show—but it makes good business sense. In business, you can't always offer the best price or the top-performing product. But you do not necessarily have to: Your value proposition can be just that people like working with you. As the legendary sports agent Bob Woolf observed, "Think about it: Why do companies spend millions and millions of dollars on public relations and goodwill advertising to develop a nice relationship with the public? Because they want to do business. They want to create a nice atmosphere. They do it because it works."

To share or not to share

We can't uncover common interests if we are too protective of information and think that our only objective is to stand our ground. When people approach negotiation as cutthroat competition, their inclination is to hold all of their information close, as if they're playing a card game and don't want to let their opponent in on their strategy. I don't advocate sharing every thought and number in your head, but this general approach of controlling information is problematic. It creates an environment of hostility and paranoia instead of one of openness. This is also the reason I don't like silent auctions. Deals are all about conversation and human connection, and a silent auction eliminates that. If you're not talking, then all you can do is limit the conversation to money and pricing. There are no shades of gray, no room for creative thinking. It goes only in two directions. More or less—up or down. Auctions eliminate innovation and collaboration. This may make for a very efficient process but it hardly makes for one that produces maximum, long-term value.

Similar difficulties apply to negotiation by email, something most of us do all the time. With a global economy where we're often thousands of miles from the person we're negotiating with, it makes sense to use technology, but I also feel strongly that if you must negotiate over email, make it a priority to first meet the other party face-to-face to share information and get to know each other. If that isn't possible, then try Skype or some other means that will allow you to *see* one another as you glean additional information with face-to-face communication. If given a choice between email and texting, always email. With texting even more information is lost, and the more we cut away human contact, the more we open the doors to miscommunication.

Glean as much information as you can, and all the while, assume abundance, which sets a tone of forthrightness and transparency. You can learn more about the other person's interests, which gives you more options to work with in a negotiation. You don't want to give away *everything*, though, so be thoughtful about what you share and what you don't.

Before a negotiation, think through what information you have, and ask, "What will happen if I share this? Will this piece of information help me or hurt me?" In more instances than not, people tend to hide information that, even if revealed, wouldn't hurt them and in fact can help them by buying them goodwill. They just think about things from a limited perspective, assuming that information held close gives them power, and/or that anything they share will somehow be used against them.

In 2000, Ursula Burns was not yet CEO of Xerox, but she was integral to turning the struggling company around. In a digital age where a company known for producing and maintaining photocopies could have become obsolete, Ursula and then CEO Anne Mulcahy had a hefty job in front of them. They needed to outsource their manufacturing in order to cut costs, but in order to do so, Ursula needed the buy-in of the Xerox union. Not an easy negotiation, as the outsourcing would mean cutting jobs and lots of them. Burns approached the negotiation with the four-thousand-employee union with transparency. "I told them the truth, in as much detail as I could, about what was happening," Burns told *Fast Company* of the meeting. Anne Mulcahy said, "She literally convinced the union that it was going to be either some jobs or no jobs. For anyone. It was survival. There was no other way." Burns thought through the information she had, understood it couldn't hurt her, and used it to garner goodwill.

Consider another example, this time a train company negotiating with its passengers for loyalty and for help in keeping the trains clean. A sign in the train bathroom read: "We know you are not happy with the cleanliness of our bathrooms. We are looking for solutions and taking interim steps like having more staff come aboard at various stops to clean them. Meanwhile, we would like to ask for your help in keeping the bathroom clean for the next guest." I was struck by this sign because it was so honest. The dog-cone inclination would be "Everything is fine here! Our passengers love us, and they even love our bathrooms!" Well, that wasn't the case. Passengers weren't happy, the train company knew it, and the passengers knew it. What's the point in hiding that information? Instead, why not reveal it to strengthen the relationship?

I almost always encourage proactively sharing market information and objective data (i.e., Kelley Blue Book values or Multiple Listing Service [MLS] data). This is information people will be able to find or have before they arrive and confirm when they leave the negotiation. If you neglect to share it—or worse, lie about it—they will recognize that you weren't forthcoming, or that you weren't knowledgeable. This will not bode well for either the chance of them negotiating with you again or your reputation generally in the long term. In the short term, it makes you appear ill-informed or shady, making it much harder to navigate the conversation. In contrast, by sharing this data, you're showing your willingness to educate them and to approach the negotiation as a problem that needs to be solved. You're encouraging them to put aside their own dog cone and to talk openly. It works: Researchers have shown that people share more when others reveal sensitive information.

If nothing else, you are taking the time to educate your counterpart so that the conversation can be informed, and an informed counterpart is so much more enjoyable than an oblivious one. CarMax took this rationale and made itself into a Fortune 500 company. It approached the field of used-car sales—one famously associated with holding critical information close—and reasoned, "We want you, the consumer, to be fully informed, and we want to be completely transparent." They have computers readily accessible for doing research if you haven't ahead of time. They want an educated consumer, believing that it saves time and encourages goodwill for everyone. CarMax recognizes that with the widespread availability of information, period, it's not hard to be an educated consumer— it's just up to the consumer to be educated.

If there is information you know you don't want to share, think carefully about how to deflect your counterpart if she asks for it. For instance, if someone asks, "What's your bottom line?" you can say, "I don't want to spend more than . . ." Which, as I already covered, is not the same at all as giving your bottom line. Research backs up the idea that if someone is an eloquent sidestepper, the listener doesn't even notice that they've deflected the question. Deflecting unwelcome questions is not something that comes easily to everyone—it's a learned skill. Just watch any politician being interviewed on a morning news show to see the dance in action. Some can evade questions by sticking to their talking points in such a blatant way that you wonder why the interviewer is even there—the politico is just giving a stump speech. Others softshoe around a firm answer with such deftness that you may have to watch the segment two or three times before recognizing that they haven't in fact answered the question at all. Jake Tapper made a name for himself because he wouldn't allow Donald Trump to deflect. "That's great," Tapper would say in response to a nonanswer, "but can you answer the question?" If worst comes to worst, and you're talking with a Jake Tapper who isn't abiding by your deflection, you can always say, "I'm not ready to answer that right now. Can we come back to it? I'd like to think about it a bit more." Find what works for you—there's no one right way to withhold strategic information.

When it comes to information sharing, I recommend, at least at first, giving more information than feels wholly comfortable. By overcorrecting those first natural, protective inclinations, you'll get to a place where you're more comfortable and feel more in control of the process. Being less afraid will help you think more rationally about what you should share and what you shouldn't.

Assume abundance to conquer fear

The most common refrain I hear when I reconnect with my former students is that assuming abundance gave them the greatest leverage of all, because it let them know they could walk away from a bad deal, a bad client, even a bad relationship. As Benjamin Franklin said, "Necessity never made a good bargain."

Take Linda Schlesinger-Wagner, the founder of Skinnytees.

Critical to her early success was the fact that QVC picked up her product and it sold well for the company. Linda worked with three different buyers during the company's five years with QVC and generally had similar contracts with all of them. Then a new buyer, whom I will call Stephanie, came in and changed the rules of engagement. Stephanie was hungry and wanted to make a name for herself. She presented a fee structure and return-rate metric to Linda that would have had Skinnytees taking on an inordinate amount of risk, such that there was a good chance Skinnytees would lose money on the deal. Linda tried to work it out with the new buyer, explaining her predicament and that the buyer's predecessors had all been willing to work *with* Skinnytees to come up with a deal that worked for everyone. Not so from this buyer. She would not negotiate.

So Linda had a decision to make: continue working with the behemoth that was responsible for a large percentage of Skinnytees sales, but at what could be a loss? Or pursue other areas of business? As Linda explains it: "I said, 'We love you and we're not happy that we have to part ways. And your customer isn't going to be happy.'" She walked away. "It was a game changer for us. Scary like I can't believe. And we were sweating it. But it made us grow in so many ways. Now I'm not dependent on any one buyer. I have to be dependent on lots of different ways of doing business today. In the old days I would have thought, let's do the deal. But I believe in my line. I can walk away from a deal and I did. And now QVC has come back and renegotiated."

Linda also had to walk away from Dillard's, another company she loved working with. Skinnytees was in forty-seven Dillard's stores nationwide when Linda saw that Dillard's had started putting the product in the underwear department, hanging between bras and panties. She really didn't like the look, which suggested Skinnytees was a lower-market brand than it was. "We met with one of the head managers and I said, 'This looks horrible—what can we do?' She told me to ask for our own kiosk. But Dillard's said no. They were great to work with, but we had to pull away—it wasn't good for our brand to be displayed like that." Linda left the relationship on good terms, which allowed her to return years later with a new idea for the product presentation that would make sense for everyone.

Dana Sicko had a similar experience with her juice company, Gundalow. Every juice company tries to be cheaper and cheaper in order to make grocery stores happy. And for a time Dana tried, too. "Then I thought, why am I trying to make these grocery stores happy who aren't good partners to work with anyway?" She described having a moment of feeling total empowerment, of recognition that she should move in a positive direction that made sense for *her*. "We can't apologize for being who we are. So we were like, we're going to sell to boutique hotels and high-end restaurants." Gundalow is going to be profitable this year, which is a pretty big accomplishment for the juice industry. "I can negotiate every part of my business," she said. "We're going to find good people and negotiate with *them*."

Jessica Johnson helms her family's private security business and was recently in the tough spot of losing one of her company's largest contracts. "One of the first things I did when I learned this relationship was ending is that I called our bankers. I said, 'All of our business we projected isn't going to happen.'" The bank, predictably, said she needed to give them a plan of what lay ahead. "I put pen to paper," she said, and it allowed her to maintain a mindset of abundance, even in the wake of this bad news. "Say we lose twenty people. We've still got a hundred. When I counted things up

I was reminded that there are eight thousand security companies in the United States and ninety-five percent make less than five million a year." (Johnson Securities is one of the top 5 percent.) She recognized, too, that less than 13 percent of women-owned businesses bring in more than $1 million in revenue. (She is in that 13 percent.) "When I realized that," she said, "I saw that I am a unicorn. Even when we take all of that business off the table, I'm still up there." Jessica's mind-set of abundance allowed her to go back to her bank with confidence and to approach new potential business with that same confidence.

Negotiation like this can also happen almost completely internally. Consider the negotiation Anna went through in her own mind. Anna was contemplating leaving her job in a marketing department. She hadn't gotten a raise in three years, nor, according to her boss, was a raise on the horizon. She considered going freelance, but there were many valid reasons to fear making the change. She would not have a guaranteed salary. She might have trouble finding clients. She would have to pay for her own health insurance. All of these reasonable fears prevented her from pushing back on her boss, because she felt she had no leverage. She couldn't leave.

When she negotiated with a mind-set of abundance, however, she recognized she could indeed leave. There were a dozen people she knew she could contact to seek freelance work. She wouldn't need as many clients because her hourly rate, working for herself, would be more than her hourly rate as an employee. There were other reasons to feel legitimately confident about the decision to go freelance: Her work quality was higher than that of some of her colleagues, and she'd be able to differentiate herself; she'd be able to go after different sorts of clients, doing things that paid more but that her company didn't do; and she could always do temp work in case of a workflow rut. And so she did, finally, walk away. And sure enough, though it wasn't seamless, there was enough work to go around.

No one who knows me would describe me as a bubbling well of optimism, and yet I recognize on a very intellectual level that when we believe in possibility, when we believe in abundance, we are rewarded. This is true when we negotiate with others, and it's an approach that works with the world at large. I believe that it's assuming abundance that gets us *beyond* yes.

Years ago, I had a great job with the U.S. Agency for International Development (USAID). It was customary for the organization to put on one or two big events at the UN General Assembly meetings in September. Shortly after I started my job as a senior advisor for sport for development there, I attended a meeting where we discussed what kind of megaevent we might orchestrate. I knew very little about such things, but I raised my hand and suggested we throw a sports event. "I can bring in all these big names," I said. "It could be exciting, and a great way to elevate our platform and reach people in a different kind of way." Within a week, I had the go-ahead.

What I didn't realize was that putting on an event of this magnitude was a huge undertaking. We had only about a month, celebrity guests to confirm, invitations to send, details to coordinate, and logistics to problem-solve for an event that would take place in New York but that we were planning from D.C. The month was exhausting but exhilarating. In the end, it all came together and the attendees raved about it.

The longer I worked at USAID, the more I realized what a big accomplishment our sports event was. I hadn't been afraid because I didn't know what I should be afraid of. I didn't know about bureaucratic obstacles, so I didn't let worrying over them stop me from thinking big. Years later, as I became more and more entrenched in the bureaucracy of the development space, it became harder for me to think expansively as I'd done when I suggested the sports event. To this day, when I realize that I am using a scarcity mind-set, I try to think back to the mind-set I'd had at the beginning of my tenure to recapture the person I'd been. I always want to be that person—the one who doesn't set limits but rather who thinks, *Why not?*

When I catch myself thinking that something can't be done—be it finding a reasonable price for a hotel or my ability to make a deadline—I often think of that woman at the jury duty scheduling desk. I imagine her impassive shrug and how easy it seemed for her to say no. She did me a favor, really. (Okay, maybe I wouldn't go that far.) I have an image of what I *don't* want to be, of how I *don't* want to think, about how I *don't* want to operate whether I'm negotiating with myself or anyone else. And then I simply take off my blinders and put my mind to the task of imagining what's possible.

CHAPTER 9

claiming your power

I n the film *Erin Brockovich*, a single mom with no law degree (played by Julia Roberts) works with her boss (a lawyer) to go after Pacific Gas and Electric (PG&E) for contaminating water and thereby poisoning its inhabitants. When three polished PG&E attorneys arrive at her small firm to meet with Erin's boss, Brockovich recruits two office workers to sit in on the meeting, so it will be four against three. The office workers don't say or do anything, nor do they need to, because their purpose is to show that the small firm will not be outnumbered or intimidated.

Most people think that leverage has everything to do with money or the amount of resources you have. But as this scene suggests, leverage is all about perception. It's about the way you bring yourself to the table. If you believe in your power, you reflect your power. For this reason, I think of Chapter 9 as the inverse of Chapter 1. In Chapter 1, I wrote about how telling ourselves stories that sell us short can hurt us in negotiation. In this chapter, I write about the opposite phenomenon—how, when we truly understand our power, we have leverage.

Sarah Farzam, the Iranian, Mexican, and Jewish founder of Bilingual Birdies, shared in Chapter 1 that she once found negotiation intimidating. Not only was she a minority woman, but she was much younger than many of the people she was doing business with. It wasn't until she understood her power that she recognized her leverage. "When I negotiate against a white man who might be older, who is representing say ten preschools together, I don't have this thing I used to have where I would paralyze a bit and do whatever I could to not talk about the money," she said. Instead, she focuses on how negotiating is in her blood, how she grew up watching her dad negotiate at Rite Aid when he was just buying toiletries, how she comes from a rich Iranian culture of merchants, going back to the beginning of civilization. "I can use that," she said. She also has the superpower of being able to relate to pretty much anyone, in large part because of her diverse heritage. Now in a negotiation, she tells herself, "Even though I'm Mexican and Iranian and a woman, I have nothing less than you have . . . I might even have more."

Mary Ellen Slayter went through the same type of evolution in her outlook. Her small content marketing company counts as its clients some of the biggest companies in the world. "The natural place for me would be to feel like they have all the power and I have none, right?" she said. That mind-set would enable them to kill her margins—and, ultimately, her business. But then she had a realization. "They wouldn't be calling me if they didn't need me, and even with the big difference with the size of the companies, it doesn't mean I don't have power. I actually have a tremendous amount of power."

Mary Ellen's company does a lot of writing, a notoriously

low-paid skill. She said sometimes she'll encounter people who think that writers are a dime a dozen, and she'll get that niggling feeling in the back of her brain that she is so lucky to be a well-paid writer. "But I'm not a writer," she said, "I'm actually a business strategist who uses content to solve business problems."

Her power is evident whenever she sits down with clients—and if it's not, she makes it so. In a recent contract negotiation with an international events company, she was pretty blunt, explaining that other than herself, there were only two others who did comparable work. "These are my competitors," she said. "They are both competent, and should you find them to be a better fit for your needs, here's their number. I know them both." Her revenue is up 40 percent since her evolution. "I know exactly where I stand and I know who I'm interchangeable with and who I'm not," she said, and that's made all the difference.

This chapter highlights the many different ways people come to understand their power and claim their leverage. Far from a one-size-fits-all prescription, power is unique to each individual and requires self-awareness to identify. Scores of myths and epic stories, from Black Panther to Wonder Woman to the Hunger Games, use this tension of the main character seeking their power as their driving force. Finding it is their hero's journey.

Embracing difference

Sallie Krawcheck has some pretty impressive credentials. She ran Smith Barney, Merrill Lynch Wealth Management, U.S. Trust, and Citi Private Bank, and was CFO of Citigroup. In the overwhelming male realm of Wall Street, she kicked ass as one of the few women. As she sees it, and as she tells it in her book *Own It: The Power of*

Women at Work, she has come to see that she succeeded not despite her gender but because of the strength of her most female qualities.

Women have distinct strengths, she argues. Men do, too, she is quick to point out, and indeed her perspective isn't one of male-bashing but of plugging diversity. But women tend to be more risk averse, she says, and risk aversion makes for stronger companies and better decisions. Women are skilled at managing complexity. They are more relationship-focused, they think longer-term, they prize a learning mind-set, and they value meaning at work. Each of these particularly "female" skills made her very good at what she did. For instance, her outlook on risk led her, early in her career as a research analyst, to call out the subprime lending practices in one of her reports, which she titled, "Whoa, Nellie!" This wasn't in 2008 but in 1994, and her willingness to write about it was explained to her as a career killer. Though there were many causes of the financial crisis of 2008, Krawcheck sees the dearth of diverse voices in the room like hers as a central factor. Most of the decision makers on Wall Street, she said, were "people who had worked together for years, went to the same universities, sent their kids to the same schools, attended the same training programs, dined at the same restaurants, got promoted together, vacationed together, played tennis together, drank together, and sat on charitable boards together." Her very difference, her very female approach to risk aversion, was what set her apart.

Krawcheck believes her focus on relationships has made her better at asking for money, as she is able to see the bigger picture from all sides—a point integral to Chapter 5 of this book. When she was CEO at the research firm Sanford Bernstein, her focus on relationships also made her recognize that the firm could not authentically serve their clients because they had two sets of clients—investing clients and corporate clients—whose interests were inherently in conflict. Although most research departments in the industry did advise both, she recommended withdrawing from the investment banking business so they could truly serve investment clients. When the Internet bubble burst, most of the competition were slapped with hundreds of millions of dollars in regulatory fines. Krawcheck, in contrast, was featured on the cover of *Fortune* with the headline *The Last Honest Analyst*.

Her relationship focus also cost her, and dearly. Sanford Bernstein lost money for years before the wisdom of her decision was clear. And when she was at Citigroup, she was fired after she pushed hard to reimburse some of their clients' investment losses after Citigroup miscalculated risk on a group of investments. "I became obsessed, totally consumed with thinking about the clients whom we had let down," she said of the time. "The clients whom we had built relationships with, who had trusted us to make the right investment decisions for them. And when I couldn't think about them anymore, I thought about the long-term harm that we were doing to our business. We had shaken those clients' confidence in us, so why would they ever want to invest their hard-earned dollars with us again?"

But Krawcheck's prioritization of the long term also has meant she's landed now in a place that's far better, as the founder of a digital investment platform for women, Ellevest, that is fulfilling and successful. She was fired, she came to see, for the same things that have also served her and will continue to serve her. "I was fired for being different, for challenging the majority opinion, for speaking up, for daring to go against the grain . . . for calling out the risk, prioritizing the long term, and for putting client relationships ahead of the short-term bottom line."

Women *are* different, she says. "And therein lie our greatest strength and competitive advantage in the modern workplace. . . . [I]t's us women deciding to celebrate rather than apologize for all the amazing unique qualities that we bring to the table—and to give ourselves permission to act like our true selves at work."

When we harness the potential of our difference, our story is one of power, not of lack. Former Xerox chief Ursula Burns was born a poor, African American female. Some said that meant she had three strikes. But as she told *Time*, "I grew up as an engineer in math and science, where it is mostly men. Mostly white men. . . . Again, difference is generally better. So you take the gender and the race differences and use them as a strength. They become a positive. You can perform as well as they can perform—or better—and you will be noticed. You have to have a continued focus and not bow to the many, many, many headwinds, but you can use them as an advantage."

Storytelling and persuasion

In a popular exercise I do in some of my classes, I give each student a paper clip and they have to trade it up over a period of several hours. To get them in the spirit, I show them a news clip of a Canadian man, Kyle MacDonald, who traded a paper clip all the way up to a house. When I tell them the kinds of objects that former students have traded up for—a mini fridge, a printer, and a trombone—they don't believe it's possible. Then I set them loose for just two hours, encouraging them to go around campus and negotiate in a way that fits their style.

My student Dylan Reim thought about how Kyle MacDonald had been successful. He hadn't really just traded a paper clip—he'd become a news sensation when he got to the point of trading for a snowmobile, and so everyone wanted to be a part of the excitement.

It was no longer about the object but about the story. Well, Dylan could do that. He came from a theatrical family that loved to dress up and stage elaborate Halloween productions. He worked for the school newspaper, so he was accustomed to organizing a narrative. Dylan could play a part, and he could welcome people to be a part of the story.

He created a Facebook page, dressed in an over-the-top sequined jacket, and set up a trading post in the middle of campus that the Facebook page directed people to. He made a sign from materials he had around his apartment, but that was it.

"I started getting a couple of people I'd never met, who thought, *I want to be on that page*," Dylan said. "That was exactly what I wanted. And the fact that I was having fun with it made me able to do it a lot better. I don't think if I were calling friends saying, 'Can I trade up?' it would have worked as well. I had to feel like I wasn't tricking others into working with me. Other people can get value for the exchange. They can see me as an equal, that I'm giving them something—they get to be part of it."

Dylan succeeded in this activity, ultimately trading up for a whiskey glass laser-etched with a mountain range, in large part because he understood his power—he could be theatrical and make people feel like part of a story. He used that power as leverage. He wasn't asking for something for nothing; he was extending an invitation to be a part of something fun and quirky. He had something valuable to offer, and he used it.

The power of problem solving

My student Bradley—who owns and operates an event space in New Orleans—came to see me after class one day to say he was reluctant to break out of the fixed pricing structure used in his business. He had a quick, short sales cycle that he said worked for him—customers could clearly see a set menu of services and choose from it. Wham, bam, done. He didn't think my emphasis on information exchange, on the importance of empathizing with the customer, applied to his company.

"I see it differently," I said. There was so much potential with Bradley. He was an incredible "people person"—that much was clear. His classmates adored him, and he was always able to get great information whenever he was bargaining. He knew he was good at information exchange, he just didn't believe that power could be harnessed to help his business. I encouraged him to spend more time up front getting to know his customers so that he could differentiate their needs and interests more effectively. I told him to leave behind his one-size-fits-all pitch, to approach every client with curiosity, as a problem solver and visionary. Bradley had reservations, so I asked what he had to lose. Like so many others in his class, he worked constantly, taking time from his family, and felt exhausted, stretched, and like he was running in place. Plus, if Bradley couldn't grow his business, he put himself at risk for the next market downturn. He made a commitment to try.

Following our after-class discussion, Bradley got a call from prospective clients wanting to throw a bat mitzvah party for their daughter. He invited them in to tour his space and decided he would be more curious and spend more time with them. He asked all of his usual questions about the party itself, but he slowed down and made an effort to get to know them. The parents were both doctors who worked very hard. The dad was from Florida, and the mom was German. "It was amazingly easy and interesting," Bradley said about learning more of the family's story. The party was to be a Hollywood-themed bat mitzvah for their daughter, who as it happened went to school with Bradley's son. Bradley also learned that the family had attended other bar and bat mitzvahs at his event space, and how convenient it was since it was only seconds from their temple—a fact Bradley knew but hadn't before considered a huge benefit.

The mom explained that the daughter had a grand vision of the night, but the parents were so busy with work-related travel that they couldn't themselves put together all that their daughter was dreaming of, unless Bradley could do it for them. "This is when it became even more fun and rewarding," Bradley reported to me later. "At my core, I love to help people and I love cool new things. I will pour myself into making this amazingly unique experience happen for people." This was his power. "They always love the outcome and are very thankful, but the problem is I have not always considered myself, my time, my creative value, as valuable."

Being curious allowed Bradley to humanize the interaction and not approach it as just another transaction. Through this process, he realized that he was a partner in a shared goal. Once it came time to provide them a cost estimate, he gave them a much higher opening offer than he would have otherwise, talking himself out of second-guessing himself or "anticipating their pushback" and focusing instead on what it would truly cost to give them the caliber of event that they wanted with all the bells and whistles.

Bradley could have put on a perfectly acceptable bat mitzvah that he made a small profit on. Instead he created a one-of-a-kind masterpiece centered on an exuberant young woman, whose love and passion for Hollywood were transformed into a custom-designed experience for her family and friends to enjoy. "When I gave the quote," Bradley said, "the mom booked on the spot, leaving me knowing that they had that extra money for us to develop this great theme, and the satisfaction to know that individuals are motivated by more than money." Saving money was not his clients' interest—making their daughter happy was. Given their lack of time, it was easy to make the hiring decision and book the event. Bradley's "ask" wasn't out of line but rather perfectly reasonable. He hadn't been greedy by any stretch of the imagination. He had just finally determined what his services and skills were worth.

Bradley's leverage only grew from there. He started attending Seth Godin marketing seminars, which highlight empathy, and he doubled down on his company's focus on it. "I started noticing that brides were emailing me at one forty-five, two, three in the morning, requesting to see the space. Well, obviously I wasn't going to get out of bed and show them at that time, but I started thinking more deeply about why they were thinking about this at two in the morning, what it was they wanted to know, and how I could help them." He wanted to make the whole process easier for them, so he decided to invest in a virtual tour with audio that brides and grooms could check out at any time that suited them, or whenever nervousness and insomnia hit.

"Some people might approach their business thinking, 'How do I make this easier on myself?' and avoid the harder clients," Bradley said. "But I think, no, it's my magic sauce to make it easier on the client. That's the differentiator with my company. And I love it if they're tough—because I try hard, and so I get to show myself as above the competition," he explained. It's worked. His bookings last year were his best ever, and he's set to be up 35 percent over that in the year to come.

The enduring power of authenticity

When Sebastian Jackson, whom I introduced in Chapter 2, finally persuaded Wayne State University to let him open a barbershop on campus (after three tries!), his predominant feeling was gratitude.

The way he saw it, he was someone who cut hair and wanted to open a barbershop, and he was happy to finally have the opportunity.

Part of his business plan from the beginning included bringing in interesting speakers to liven the place up and to build connections among the community who used the barbershop.

A friend of his commented, "This is a black barbershop." Sebastian said it wasn't, but his friend insisted. "I thought it was degrading our culture," Sebastian said, when he thought of the stereotype of the African American barbershop as a place of community gossip. "I was looking to elevate the barbershop."

Sebastian ran from the stereotype, instead focusing on bringing through the door all kinds of people with all kinds of hair to be cut. By the second or third year of business, though, Sebastian understood the value he was bringing. "I was almost disrespecting the barbershop culture that's been built," he said. "As we grew, I saw we were bringing interesting people to Wayne State. We were giving people access to interesting people who would come to our barbershop." He realized his shop, The Social Club, was playing a real role in reviving Detroit. "I realized that I have value to add—I'm black in a city that's eighty-five percent black." And although The Social Club welcomes all customers, he realized, "This is a black barbershop because it's a black-owned barbershop."

His outlook has given him a lot of leverage in his business as he looks to grow and expand. "The people who are doing all this development [in Detroit] are looking to be inclusive. I'm from Flint, grew up in Detroit, so now they *need* that. They *need* The Social Club." The very thing he was afraid of accepting, which was the authenticity of experience he could offer customers, is now his great leverage.

I've seen so many people, like Sebastian, who struggle against a part of themselves that they've been conditioned to think is a weakness, when in fact it's a strength. The racial baggage regarding the "barbershop" is an example of this; another is the trait of introversion.

Susan Cain, an introvert like me, worked at a law firm and—believe it or not—was a negotiations consultant before turning to writing and lecturing. She noticed that introverts were constantly being told to get out there, to be around people, to be social, to be—in effect—something that they weren't. Her TED Talk on the subject and her book, *Quiet: The Power of Introverts in a World That Can't Stop Talking*, were immediate hits. It turns out there are a lot of us who don't see our introversion as a superpower but would very much like to. And we should. Introverts notice things about people, they are careful, they are excellent listeners, and they think deeply. All of these traits are brilliant in a negotiation.

The same is true for emotionality. When Julia signed up for my negotiations class, for instance, she was sure it would be a struggle. She had worked as a consultant before returning to business school at Wharton, and from her mentors and her work experience, she had become convinced that showing emotion and revealing vulnerability signaled weakness. The problem, as Julia saw it, was that she was a naturally empathetic, open person. She felt she would have to bury those aspects of her personality when she took my class.

Indeed, on the first day it probably seemed like she would. Without much preamble, I sent everyone off for a mock negotiation, and then when they returned I put the results on the board. Julia hadn't done well. "The guy I went up against pulled the wool over my eyes," she remembered. "Everyone was trying to win—everyone was viewing negotiation that way. I remember coming back to the room and being so embarrassed and thinking, how am I going to get through this class? I was too nice, I was gullible."

Soon after, though, I talked to the class about Brené Brown's book *Daring Greatly: How the Courage to Be Vulnerable Transforms the Way We Live, Love, Parent, and Lead*, which focuses on the power of vulnerability. I connected it to negotiation, explaining that being open and telling someone how you feel in a negotiation can be a great source of power. "It resonated with me," said Julia, "this assertion that being vulnerable can be powerful. Because vulnerability is the stuff of relationships, and relationships are the point of negotiation."

Julia went from viewing negotiation as an isolated, scary activity to grasping that negotiation is about emotional intelligence, being open with yourself and others about what you want and why. Now that she had the permission to be who she was, she realized that it was actually her greatest source of power. That doesn't mean she "word-vomits," as she put it. Words matter, and she is thoughtful about what she shares with others and how. But she is more likely to be forthcoming about what is hard and what isn't. Now that she's returned to her job as a consultant, she said, "Selling projects to clients, I see now, is a negotiation. We scope a piece of work to help them, and then we need to work with them to jointly determine what is most important to them, how we should tailor our focus and our team to best help them. We have to make trade-offs and be clear about expectations—what we will and won't do. It's about zeroing in on what they really need, and it doesn't always mean that we just do more for them. We are not afraid to tell them that something they've asked us to help with isn't our area of expertise or isn't the best use of their money. Being open, being vulnerable, and communicating more through the process helps us do the work we're best positioned to do and helps them make wise investments. I don't go into these conversations stressed out. We're understanding of their requirements. They're understanding of ours. What's to worry about?"

Dana Sicko, founder of Gundalow Gourmet, shared a lot of

Julia's characteristics—and her fears. "I went into business thinking, I'm a woman going into a very saturated field. I'm going to be bulldozed every time I talk to someone." Then, in class, we talked about the power of empathy to make you a phenomenal negotiator. "This was right off of a week with my therapist where we were talking about how I have a lot of empathy," Dana said. "Something I never thought would be a strength for me, I was told is. I'm emotionally intelligent, and that's intrinsic to who I am. That gave me so much confidence when I realized it was my superpower."

Ambassador Wendy Sherman wrote that in her negotiation with Iran over the country's nuclear capacity, a turning point came when frustrated tears ran down her face as she spoke to her Iranian counterparts. As she remembers, they were stunned by her emotion, because "this weeping, viscerally direct Wendy was a person they hadn't encountered." It's not that the moment changed the game they'd been locked in for months, and really, for years. "But something in the sincerity of my frustration," Wendy wrote, "the realness of the moment, broke through. . . . [T]he fact is that when we are ourselves, even if that means letting our tears flow, we can be our most powerful."

Experience matters

Glen Cutrona is an architect who's been in business for thirty years. The guy knows his way around a drafting board. Still, when meeting with prospective clients, he used to spend a lot of time *talking* about his experience, so that they would know just how qualified he was. He used to spend an inordinate amount of time agonizing over quotes, because he was afraid that if he priced something too high he would lose the customer. As a competitive guy, he desperately wanted to beat out whoever else was bidding on the job.

Glen was letting his competitors and the market define his value, a mistake. Glen had to recognize that his power was his experience. After thirty years, he knew better than most what it takes to do a job in a quality way. "There's a certain standard of care that needs to be devoted to a project," he explained. "People in the public do not know to what extent the services are. They don't know what to ask for."

He has gotten pushback from prospective clients, who will say, "Well, this other architect costs one third less than you do." Whereas in the past this would have kicked Glen's competitive nature into gear, now it doesn't. He just explains he couldn't do a job to his standards for that fee, and he explains what is required to do his work in a high-quality way. "I still want to win, but win so that it's good for everyone, including myself. I know that the list of services that I put on a job is what is needed to produce a good end product." He's not letting others place a value on him. "If you're calling our firm, I don't compromise."

Glen no longer spends time telling clients about his qualifications—instead, he asks them questions. "If you know your stuff," he said, "you don't need to explain that to people." He feels more confident, and since he is resting in his power of experience, he has all the leverage he needs.

"The results have been great," Glen said. "My firm is doing significantly better. I don't know that I'm doing much more work, but I'm pricing it correctly. We're able to service our clients. Our end result has always been good, but now it's better."

Prepare, prepare, prepare

Alan Harris owns a bridal boutique with his wife, Jeannine, and his daughter, Melissa, but he's a data guy at heart. While his daughter has more of an eye on fashion aesthetics, Alan looks carefully at their inventory and implemented a system where salespeople record not only which gowns are sold but which are tried on.

One day they got a visit from a sales rep for the line they do the most business with, and with whom they have an exclusive arrangement. "Your sales are going down," the rep said. "We're going to open up this line to a second store."

Alan and Melissa were confused. "Wait a minute," they said. "We don't see our sales going down. So what's the disconnect?"

The impasse was not resolved that day, but Alan and Melissa wrote a letter to the sales rep's boss—who, they later found out, was actually her boss's boss's boss—and who acted on it quickly. The company executives invited them for an in-person meeting. Melissa brought a simple but thorough chart that demonstrated their sales—that all three lines from this designer had gone up, and that their dresses were getting tried on 90 percent of the time. In a simple format, Melissa was able to show precisely which dresses were being tried on, and that of the top twenty dresses tried on in the past six months, eighteen were from this designer.

"We don't see how you can say that they're not going up," Melissa said.

The design executives were appropriately impressed, and said so. "We have some graphs to show you too, but we can't explain them as well as you can explain yours."

Melissa and Alan were then able to move the discussion toward what the real objective was. "What's the partnership we can do to increase sales to brides? Let's concentrate on that," Alan said, which led to a much more cooperative discussion. "We set some good mutual goals," Alan said, "and determined discounts associated with obtaining those goals. We talked about some things the design company could do to help us, like trunk shows."

The design company then aired their grievance that their labels were removed from the gowns before they were tried on. "We pay to advertise on our website to push customers to your location, and you're not featuring us by allowing our name to be in the dresses."

The two parties then turned to problem-solving this issue. The reason boutiques take labels out is that they don't want brides to find a dress they like at the boutique and spend all of the salesperson's time, but then—based on the designer and stock number—hunt around for the lowest price. Working together, they determined that going forward there was a way to take the stock number out but leave the designer name in.

"Can you put the labels back in that you've already taken out?" the design company asked.

Alan and Melissa said they couldn't, because it was too time intensive. But they suggested that the design company could send someone to their store to do it.

All in all, Alan reflected, it was a really successful negotiation because everyone left happy. And the preparation they'd done—the rich data they'd collected—gave them credibility. "We were able to present facts, not emotions or feelings. So that helped," he said. The data made clear, too, that a lot of designer companies sell wedding gowns. Alan and Melissa said they were actually questioning whether they should be doing 60 or 70 percent of their business with one company. "Our data gave us leverage to have that conversation."

Valuing likability

Though Chapter 2 focused on the troubles inherent in needing to be liked, there's also no denying that likability is an asset. If you're a good person, if you're kind, people will want to be around you. Likable people tend to go far in life.

I'm a big proponent of kindness for an altogether unexpected reason: I don't enjoy conflict, and whatever result I'm going for, I don't want to get there having had a knife fight. I want to get there in a way that doesn't make me feel like I've fought a war. I want to get there in a way that's not gruesome. You can put in the effort to keep a conflict going, or you can think to yourself: *You know what? Honey is just going to attract the bees.*

There may be no better venue for practicing kindness and likability than at an airport—particularly after a stressful travel experience. I was recently at the Providence airport, a bit stressed because I'd just missed a flight. I had a negotiation ahead of me: I needed to talk to the customer service agent about what could be done, and hopefully I wouldn't eat the entire cost of the ticket. I waited in line behind these two women who were taking turns yelling at the agent. The agent looked tired. When it was my turn, I went up and said, "So I missed that flight. I just want to know what my options are. And I don't know what just happened with the people in front of me, but I'm sorry you have to put up with it. We can't blame you."

The agent smiled and sighed. She printed me a ticket for the next flight and said, "Here's your ticket. Come back in two hours to board." It's true that she might have charged me the full fare, but it didn't matter. My strategy of communicating kindly and respectfully was still better than any alternative. I felt good about giving her the respect that I felt she had been robbed of by the customers before me. And I was genuine—hers was not a job I would want!

John Lynch, whom I wrote about in Chapter 5, has long had a reputation for his likability. Although he was a madman on the field as an NFL safety, fiercely competitive and unwilling to take crap from anyone, off the field he was known as a sweetheart. He was all too happy to delegate negotiation responsibilities to his agent. He always felt that certain people were made to negotiate, and he wasn't one of those people. "I wasn't a hard-line negotiator," he said. "I would always give in early and my agent would be like, 'John, you have big leverage. You're at the top of your game. You're the best safety in the National Football League.'

"What I did know is what made me happy," he explained, "and I'd say, 'Hey, I like playing for this organization. I like certainty. I know that. Let's take the deal.' I'd always leave him disappointed, but we always did kind of believe, whether it was going to buy a car or whatever, that maybe I was too nice of a personality to be a skilled negotiator."

But when he took my class, John killed it. He recognized that people with "nice" personalities could do well using just that trait and finding ways everyone could win. "I would say, from that class on, I've always had more confidence in those situations," he said. Now that he's the general manager of the 49ers and negotiates with agents constantly, he sees that directness and likability go hand-in-hand. "I used to think being direct was being confrontational," he said. But now he recognizes its great value. "So many people posture," he said, "and the guys who just say, 'Hey, John, this is what it's going to take' are the ones I enjoy dealing with most. You learn to trust certain ones."

Lynch felt this approach was particularly effective in the franchise's signing of quarterback Jimmy Garoppolo. "We got on a plane and I just kind of started the meeting with [his agent] Don Yee by saying, 'Listen, Jimmy hasn't played a lot of football, but we have gotten to a point where we really believe he is our guy. We have the ability to franchise Jimmy and play that game, but that's not what I want. I want to get a deal done, and Don, here's my promise. We're not going to come in low, so that you can counter high. We're going to come in strong.'

"That's my style," Lynch said. "If I have a style of negotiation, it's *let's not beat around the bush*. I'll say, 'We're going to come strong and I want you to know that going in. Not saying that there's not going to be any room for wiggle, because obviously, that's a part of negotiation, but we're not going to insult each other's integrity, intelligence. We're going to take a hard attempt at getting this done.'

"In the past," Lynch went on, "I would have thought, *Oh. That's too bold to try to do that*. But what I've found is, it's effective, because there's no gray area for anyone."

That's not to say that Lynch isn't aware that his reputation for likability might encourage some to take advantage. Sometimes people try, he said. "You have to be willing to say, 'No. I communicated exactly what I told you. I understand you're trying to do a job, but I want to be very clear, this is where we're at.' It's like your kids. If you say you're going to do something, you better be willing to do it."

For someone like Lynch, finding ways to connect with those he's negotiating with is pretty straightforward—they always will have a passion for football in common. It might surprise you, though, just how important finding common ground is. In his book *Influence: The Psychology of Persuasion*, seminal psychologist and thinker Dr. Robert Cialdini emphasizes how important similarity is in likability. The more time you spend with someone, the more familiar you become, the more you see you have in common, and the more you *like* them. In a study of MBA students, some were told to get straight down to business in a negotiation, whereas others were told not to negotiate until they'd exchanged some personal information with the other. They were instructed to "identify a similarity you share in common, then begin negotiating." The straight-down-to-business group came to a resolution 55 percent of the time, which isn't awful, but the friendly group? They came to a resolution 90 percent of the time, and those resolutions were more advantageous to *both* parties.

A nonprofit called PeacePlayers takes this principle and literally runs with it, as it uses sports as the common link between opposing parties. In places like Jerusalem, Jewish and Arab teenagers play on basketball teams together. In Northern Ireland, where less than 7 percent of schools integrate Catholics and Protestants, kids play sports on the same side. Ninety-one percent of them had never interacted with someone from a different background until they joined PeacePlayers, which is also active in Cyprus, South Africa, and parts of the United States. PeacePlayers is such a great reminder to me of why I love sports—it brings people together around a common cause, a universal language.

From kids to adults, from sports to nuclear war, common ground remains a powerful tool. Whenever Ambassador Sherman met with her Iranian counterparts, they could not shake her hand because they were conservative Islamists, and she was of the opposite sex. Instead of letting this be a point of division, Sherman told them that she'd grown up in an Orthodox Jewish neighborhood, where the Orthodox were not allowed to touch anyone of the opposite sex if they weren't closely related. The conversation melted a little of the ice between them. "They could see me a little better," Sherman wrote, "not just as a representative of the United States, or as an untouchable member of the opposite sex, but as a human being with a history and an appreciation for their cultural norms. After this, we still bowed instead of shaking hands, but the fact that we could not shake hands became not an obstacle but a point of commonality."

Fake it till you make it

As all experienced negotiators know, the best way to get leverage is to know you can walk away. To do this, you need to know your best alternative to a negotiated agreement, or BATNA. The stronger your

BATNA, the stronger your leverage, because you know you can walk away—you don't *need* this client or this business.

But what if you do?

If that's the case, then your mind-set is more important than your reality. If you feel that you don't have power, you need to put mind over matter and exude strength anyway. You need to fake it till you make it. Take a more direct page from Erin Brockovich's book. If you are just one attorney going up against three, you might have to change the optics a bit. This is the same reason that when you encounter a bear, you are supposed to wave your arms and make yourself look as big as possible. If you can't authentically give others the perception that you have power, then you have to use some Jedi mind tricks.

One way to do this is by acting the part, as Brockovich did. Scientific studies have shown that when you force yourself to smile, even when you're feeling like crap, you actually start to feel better because the physical act of smiling triggers a chemical reaction in the brain, releasing dopamine and serotonin. Similarly, if you behave in a dominant way even when you have no power, you actually begin to feel more powerful. It's not just fake perception anymore, it's real. Importantly, dominant behaviors are *not* shouting or bullying. Rather, they involve behaviors like making expansive gestures so you take up more space (think of bears again), speaking loudly, and being assertive. Although a study from the University of Southern California showed that this works, its authors caution that if your counterpart believes you're acting as a way to gain status, it will backfire. So use dominant behaviors with caution.

The important, groundbreaking work of Harvard research scientist Amy Cuddy showed that when you stand in a dominant posture—like putting your arms out wide or on your hips Wonder

Woman style—for two minutes, your testosterone level goes up and your cortisol (stress hormone) level goes down, giving you a sense of higher confidence and lower stress reactivity. She suggests doing it for two minutes in private before going into that negotiation, job interview, or any situation where you fear being evaluated. Cuddy emphasizes the importance not of faking it till you make it but faking it till you *become* it. "We convince by our presence," she wrote, quoting Walt Whitman, then added, "and to convince others we need to convince ourselves."

Another Jedi mind trick is to simply imagine that you have more power. This takes the power of positive thinking to another level, but one that is grounded in research. In a series of experiments, those who were trying to sell a CD but had just one (weak) offer were asked to *imagine* having a strong offer. They performed as well as the sellers who weren't imagining it but actually did have a strong alternate offer. Those who didn't have a strong alternative offer and who didn't imagine having one did not do as well.

You never want to go into a negotiation feeling desperate, or that you need that deal to feel complete. That deal will not define you. Sometimes you fight that inclination by looking inward and embracing your power—be it vulnerability, like the consultant Julia, or creative partnership, like event space owner Bradley. And sometimes when the chips are obviously stacked against you, you must dig even deeper, finding the grain of belief and standing on it strongly . . . even if for the time being, you're standing on just one foot.

Resting in your power: Negotiating with bullies

My students constantly ask, "What if I'm negotiating with a liar?" "What if I'm trying to make a connection and the person rebuffs my attempts?" "What if all he does is shout (or tweet)?" They are accustomed to a world where it seems like bullying strategies *work*, even if the academic research, the world's foremost experts on negotiation, and history itself say otherwise.

The thing is, there's no one way to negotiate with a bully, and in all likelihood, it will take building on all that's come in this book so far and trying several strategies. Do always bring open-mindedness and empathy to the process. The more you can understand where the bully is coming from, what her interests are, and why she behaves the way she does, the more insight you have into how to handle her. For instance, if she bullies because she is insecure, part of your task will be to help her feel she's done well even if you've come away having met all of your objectives. Do still try to disarm her, because even if charm doesn't work, it might, and you've got nothing to lose by trying.

If your counterpart's particular form of bullying is lying, a combination of preparation, information gathering, presence, and the emotional intelligence you're bringing to bear should tip you off. Doing your research and due diligence before coming to the table will probably alert you to the person's reputation. If, say, you are discussing the value of an object he's selling, don't take his word for what it's sold for before. Ask to see the proof or find it on your own before going into the negotiation if you can.

Take the long view. A bully ultimately earns a reputation, and people won't want to negotiate with her or do business with her at all. Remember the study I cited in Chapter 7: People are much more likely to walk away if the person they're negotiating with exhibits anger. Even if the bully *looks* like she won in the short term, as practically every Hollywood movie moralizes, we know the bully gets hers in the end.

Many voters admired President Trump for matching the bully-ing language of North Korea's Kim Jong Un on the issue of nuclear weapons testing. In an oft-cited tweet from 2018, Trump wrote: "North Korean Leader Kim Jong Un just stated that the 'Nuclear Button is on his desk at all times.' Will someone from his depleted and food starved regime please inform him that I too have a Nuclear Button, but it is a much bigger & more powerful one than his, and my Button works!" For a time, it did seem that the North Koreans tamped down their nuclear weapons testing. Trump and his sup-porters felt vindicated. As I write this, though, North Korea has just test-fired short-range missiles, overseen by Kim Jong Un. The showdown does not look likely to end anytime soon.

There are some who will insist that the only way to deal with a bully is to match him, tenor for tenor, shout for shout, punch for punch. Honestly, I just don't see the point. It's not going to make him respect you. Knowing your leverage *will*. In the end, there is no better way to negotiate with a bully than to know your own power. You can't be boxed from side to side, or cowed, if you understand your leverage. And while ultimately the bully will ultimately be knocked down a peg, whether by you or someone else, you will still be standing tall.

Jessica Johnson, the head of a security company whom I intro-duced in the last chapter, has dealt with her share of bullies. She recalled that when she hired someone from a much bigger company, the new hire confessed that when she shared her plans her former bosses had said, "You're going to work for David, you know. They're David, and we're Goliath. We're buying everyone up and we'll buy them up, too."

Jessica grinned. "I thought, wait, they must not have read the rest of the Bible, because we know how that story ends." My thoughts exactly.

CHAPTER 10

how negotiation can save democracy

I always have two TVs on in my apartment—one set to cable news, the other to ESPN. My obsession with news and politics rivals my obsession with sports. But unlike sports, the news typically brings me down (a common reaction from anyone who pays too much attention to it). It feels like one fight after another, with no one side getting through to the other. I recognize there has always been disagreement in politics. In fact, a thriving democracy *needs* opposing views. But what I see around me now isn't a healthy difference of opinion. I see people yelling through bullhorns and then putting their hands over their ears when the other side wants to talk. It's alarming and makes me think of what Abraham Lincoln once said: "America will never be destroyed from the outside. If we falter and lose our freedoms, it will be because we destroyed ourselves."

When I leave the noise of news for a while, though, and enter my classroom, I immediately feel more hopeful. As we discuss and practice principles like asking questions and listening with authentic interest, going into conversations with open minds, being present, trying to understand without judgment, and establishing commonalities, it's pretty clear that all of these skills apply to political conversations. We're not using negotiation to heal democracy, but we should.

Democrats and Republicans alike are concerned about the divisiveness in America. Our reluctance to learn from one another and our dogged opinions create more barriers and division. Our anger, pain, and disappointment only further fuel these divisions, as do our biases. We come to conversations already convinced that we know everything. This is a terrible way to coexist with one another and will never be a successful negotiation.

Of course, there's always been discord between the parties, but the divisions have grown exponentially in the past twenty-five years, and as a result very little gets accomplished on either side. The main accomplishment is a sowing of distrust and even hate for the opposition. Brett Kavanaugh won a seat on the Supreme Court by a vote of 50–48, divided by party. That's not how it used to be. In 1993, Ruth Bader Ginsburg was approved for the Court by a vote of 96–3. On the other side, Antonin Scalia was approved in 1986 by a vote of 98–0. Though Scalia and Ginsburg had very different interpretations of the law, they had a famously close friendship.

Hostility toward opposing views is one part of the problem, but so is our increasing isolation, our lack of a sense of belonging. The University of Chicago's John Cacioppo has been studying loneliness for two decades, and he says the number of people who feel lonely has steadily risen over the years—with between 11 and 20 percent reporting loneliness in the 1970s and 1980s, rising to as high as 45 percent in 2010. *Connecting* is an active practice that requires physical presence, not just hitting a like button on social media. In an increasingly disconnected world, we can't assume that social networks or anonymous comments on news outlets will do the work for us. We've got to go old school. We've got to consciously decide to engage, even when it's easier not to. We cannot afford to just communicate with those who agree and count all others out. It's true that we may not change minds. That happens with negotiations all the time—sometimes, there's no deal. But we still have to come to the table.

"Throughout American history, important strides were made because people dared to share their political views with relatives," wrote Karen Tamerius, founder of the progressive advocacy group Smart Politics. "The civil rights movement, the women's movement, the antiwar movement, the gay rights movement, the struggle for marriage equality—all gained acceptance through difficult conversations among family members who initially disagreed vehemently with one another." It's easier to talk about lighter issues, sure, but when we sidestep harder conversations, we sacrifice opportunities to move the needle, even if just marginally so.

When you put the chapters of this book, then, to the test of negotiating with your neighbors about what should be done in your community, state, and country, you will see how when we hear each other—*really* hear each other—we have a shot at moving forward together instead of staying mired in gridlock or staying isolated in our corners. This chapter isn't about who's right and who's wrong. Rather, the focus is that we've gotten to a place where we are very alone—and that is not democracy. Democracy demands that we engage and have the courage to show up. We can use the lessons of effective negotiation to help us.

Start where they are

Several of my favorite negotiation exercises test students' ability to make very hard, ethical, values-based decisions. Some require teams to choose one life over another. There are never right or wrong answers. The point, rather, is to see how a group of individuals with different life experiences, demographics, values, and communication styles can come to an agreement when the stakes are high. I touched on this subject, on the subjective meaning of *fair*, when I wrote about the lifesaving dialysis machine in Chapter 5.

In the end of that exercise, each group announces who they chose, and why. After hearing each group's decision, I ask if anyone in the group had a different perspective. In one class, I'll never forget the young woman, Carolyn, who raised her hand to say she disagreed with her team. They had chosen the child, but she felt the CEO should be saved instead. I asked her why.

"I'm from Kansas City," she said. "Jobs are so important. Especially in a community like mine that hasn't done well. This CEO is critical to that community—she's irreplaceable."

One of her classmates responded, "How do you know another CEO couldn't come in and do just as good a job?"

"Because," Carolyn argued, "*this* is the CEO who has driven the company's growth. The company is thriving because of her. She is the one who developed the jobs, she is the one who could keep people employed. And jobs in small towns are everything."

"Yeah," said another one of her classmates, "but why couldn't someone else run the company successfully so that jobs wouldn't be lost? CEOs lose their jobs all the time and are replaced by someone else, and the company's just fine."

Carolyn continued to repeat the same arguments, emphatically, and kept saying, "Yeah, but in places like Kansas City . . ."

Finally one of her classmates said, "I'm confused. There are so many other people who could do that. Haven't you been anywhere outside of Kansas City?"

Carolyn's silence spoke volumes.

This was such a powerful moment. Carolyn was from an economically struggling community with a different relationship with employment than her peers had. They couldn't make arguments that would make sense to her without first understanding where she was starting from. Tactics aside, the student who had essentially discredited Carolyn felt terrible. She was of Latin descent and had lived and traveled all around the world. She hadn't even realized what assumptions she was making about Carolyn before the words were out of her mouth. Carolyn's perspective was just so radically different from her own that she had quickly dismissed it as wrong.

In 2015, *This American Life* aired a story about people who canvassed in support of issues like gay marriage and abortion. The canvassers' approach was different than you might expect. They did not approach a voter and say, "I think you should support gay marriage and here's why." Instead, they asked questions about the voter's life. In one memorable conversation, the voter—who announced he was against gay marriage—started talking about his wife, who had died years before but whom he mourned every day. He talked about his love for her and how he wanted others to experience that kind of love, too. As the canvasser asked what his exposure to gay people had been, the voter talked about the lesbian couple who lived across the street, and how they were happy like he and his wife had been. He connected the dots himself by interacting with the canvasser—who was gay—on a very human level. When the canvasser asked him at the end of the conversation if he supported gay marriage, his answer had changed.

There is nothing about understanding another person's point of view that is easy, particularly when it comes to political conversations. For when we are emotionally, economically, politically, or socially invested in a given side, it's hard to separate emotion and stay in fact-finding mode.

Controlling emotions in political conversations

Talking about politics with someone with opposing views requires you take Chapter 7 about presence and put it on steroids. Politics is so loaded that every Thanksgiving the Internet is packed with articles titled, "Ten Ways to Survive Dinner with Your Conservative/ Liberal Family." My best advice for when you feel flooded is to take a breath and to think strategically. What will happen if you lose your temper? What will you gain? Will you change anyone's mind?

There is no part of me that thinks that controlling your emotions is easy in these circumstances. If you are Jewish, descended from Holocaust survivors, or a person of color, it feels like a jarring attack for someone to defend the 2017 racist and anti-Semitic rallies in Charlottesville. Once they make their feelings known, you are starting that conversation from a place of feeling deeply disrespected. You are hurt. You want to go on the offensive, not hear what they have to say—you think they don't deserve the respect of your attention. I don't blame you. This is a huge task.

It is remarkable what can happen, though, when you just take a breath. Heather McGhee, an African American leader of a public policy organization, was a guest on CSPAN's *Washington Journal* when Garry Civitello, a private citizen who was watching the show, called in to ask a question. "I am a white male," he said, "and I am prejudiced." Heather's eyes closed for a long moment. You can see her take a breath. Garry said, "What can I do to change? To be a bet-ter American?" As the *Upstanders* documentary series reported, Heather's response—first thanking him for his honesty, and then telling him that he should turn off the nightly news, which just re-inforces negative stereotypes; that he should read about African American history; and that he should engage with African Americans—started Garry on what Heather called "a walk." He did all she suggested and more, periodically asking her advice, and the two became friends. Granted, this conversation started from a point of concession. Garry had an openness and curiosity that he made clear from the get-go. Still, he also had deep-seated ideas that cut to the core of Heather's identity. It would have been easy for her to let the hurt take over and to blow him off. But she closed her eyes, took a breath, and welcomed him in instead.

Not everyone has prejudices as extreme as Garry's, but biases can be very deeply ingrained, and everyone has them in one form or another. Remembering this, I find, is helpful to tempering strong reactions. In Todd Rose and Ogi Ogas's book *Dark Horse: Achieving Success through the Pursuit of Fulfillment*, they make the point that even a hundred years after Copernicus shared his clear logic about why the earth orbited the sun and not vice versa, few believed it. "Assumptions are very stubborn things," they write, "particularly when they are stitched into the fabric of everyday reality." Galileo then discovered four moons orbiting Jupiter, proving Copernicus correct, but "when he invited his geocentric-minded colleagues to peer through his telescope to see the moons for themselves, many insisted they could not see what Galileo claimed they should see. Some declared it hurt their head just to look." The moral I take from this story: Bias is not about you, it's not about me, it's about all of us, and so you can't lose your mind whenever someone says something stupid, because we all do. Or, in the words of Malcolm X, "Don't be in such a hurry to condemn a person because he doesn't do what you do or think as you think. There was a time when you didn't know what you know today."

Assume you need to explain

In the movie *Hidden Figures*, based on the lives of three African American women who pushed through racism and sexism to make a mark at NASA in the 1960s, mathematician Katherine Johnson returns to the office soaking wet after a break. Her boss, irritated by her long absence, calls her to task in front of the rest of the office. Angry and fighting tears, she then gives a monologue that is arguably the most powerful in the film:

> There's no bathroom for me here. ("What do you mean there's no bathroom?") There is no bathroom. There are no colored bathrooms in this building. Or any building outside the West Campus, which is half a mile away. Did you know that? I have to walk to Timbuktu just to relieve myself. And I can't use one of the handy bikes. Picture that, Mr. Harrison. My uniform. Skirt below my knees, my heels, and a simple string of pearls. Well, I don't own pearls. Lord knows you don't pay coloreds enough to afford pearls! And I work like a dog, day and night, living off of coffee from a pot none of you wanna touch. So, excuse me if I have to go to the restroom a few times a day.

It was the first moment in the film when she did not act the part she was expected to play—that of a demure, subordinate computer (she was even called a "computer"). She was emotional, and it was personal. No one in the room with her could deny the pain. She tapped into their capacity for empathy, putting them in her high heels and asking them to imagine what her life was like.

We all must do what Katherine did. We assume that of course someone can see what we're up against as a black/white/religious/atheist/man/woman—isn't it obvious? And if they can't see, why is the onus on us to tell them? Remember, though, the illusion of transparency: the belief that what you feel (or want) is crystal clear to others, even though you have done very little to communicate it. There is reality, and then there is perception, and the two are not the same. Although of course most people working at NASA in the 1960s had to recognize that it would be hard to be an African American woman working there, until Katherine showed her humanity and put them in her shoes, they didn't connect the dots of what she was up against.

A modern example comes out of the #MeToo and feminist movements, and an increasing number of women asking to be heard. Author Kimberly Harrington wrote about the plea for understanding in *Medium*: "We—who live in these bodies and are used to holding keys clutched between fingers when walking to the car and who are used to being passed over for a promotion in favor of an incompetent male coworker who is just better at bluster—are asking our partners to assume experiences they have likely never had, and likely never will. We are asking them to be better, instantly. We are asking them to be us." Even the most caring and helpful of men may not grasp the weight of what women carry unless they are told, and they listen, and they try to empathize.

The dangers, of course, are of feeling that you do not need to explain—that you should not have to explain—or, worst of all, that it's pointless to explain because the other side "will never understand." When we take these positions, we invite a pendulum swing. We do not find common ground, because we're not even looking for it. Instead we commiserate with friends and invite in the confirmation bias we talked about in Chapter 5. And on and on the miscommunication goes.

When I watched the movie *Hotel Mumbai*, I was so struck by its handling of this issue that I scrambled around in the dark theater to find a notebook so I could jot it down. In the midst of telling a remarkable and heartwrenching story, it also demonstrates how we negotiate our biases in the most human of interaction. *Hotel Mumbai*, of course, is based on the attack of the elite hotel—a symbol of capitalism—in India in 2008. As terrorists with machine guns stormed the building, a Sikh waiter named Arjun working in the hotel restaurant managed to lead a group of guests to a safe part of the hotel. The group became more and more frightened as the death and carnage was more evident, and one older British guest became completely paranoid and her instability threatened to put them all at risk. The chef whom Arjun worked under explained that Arjun's turban made the guest uncomfortable and that he should take it off. Knowing little about the turban or why he wore it, she associated Arjun with one of the militants who had stormed the building.

Now, for Sikhs, it is not a small thing to take off a turban. Arjun was never, ever without it and clearly didn't want to remove it, but neither did he want to defy the chef or let the British woman's paranoia put their group's safety at stake. So he went over to the woman. He introduced himself. He took a picture out of his wallet of his pregnant wife and their daughter. He explained that he was a father, and that he was a Sikh. He explained that Sikhs practice peace, and explained why he wore a turban and that he had never before taken it off. He emphasized that he was a family man and wanted the group to survive, but that he recognized she was uncomfortable with what he wore on his head. He told her that since she was a guest and guests came first, that he would take it off if it would make her feel better. The woman said no. It was such a powerful negotiation, and one where had Arjun chosen not to explain himself, things could have gone much differently.

Tell stories

In the words of *Righteous Mind* author Jonathan Haidt, "The human mind is a story processor, not a logic processor."

Perhaps that's why a recommended way to increase your empathy is to read fiction. It makes sense: The phrase "lose yourself in a book" means to figuratively occupy the world and viewpoints of the characters on the page. Researchers at the New School even found that those who read literary fiction were more empathetic.

Dr. Michelle C. Pautz, a researcher out of the University of Dayton who has studied the power of film to change minds, said, "Discussing race relations/racism is still hard for Americans and an often taboo subject, but one can much more easily talk about a movie that might then lead to conversation about those more sensitive topics." Remember how when *Philadelphia* came out, starring Tom Hanks, it helped destigmatize AIDS? Part of the reason was that finally people were talking about a subject that it was much more comfortable to avoid.

The connection of all of this to negotiation is yet again empathy, the heart and soul of good negotiation practices. Stories help us humanize fraught issues, break stereotypes, and let down our protective guard, and from there we are better able to communicate. It's why, in a discussion about health care, it's more effective to tell the story of your brother who struggled to pay his medical bills when he had brain cancer than it is to quote politicians—or statistics—on either side. Or, in a conversation about gun control, to explain that you are not an advocate of people gunning others down, but that in the remote countryside where you live, police aid is not right around the corner and your gun is thus your only source of protection. Just as you are listening to their story, you must share your own.

Keep talking: Going from dispute to understanding, no matter how hard it is

I said I shy away from talking about politics in the classroom, but sometimes it comes up and the conversation needs to run its course. About a week after the horrific hate-crime killing of Jews at their synagogue in Pittsburgh's Squirrel Hill neighborhood, I taught a class in Chicago. It was a fantastic group of easygoing, intelligent, highly engaged students, and the classroom was filled with light banter all morning long. One of the students, an older Latina woman named Sofia, caught my attention because she was just so outgoing. She ran a successful staffing firm and was clearly quite the saleswoman, too—she was charming and engaged everyone in conversation.

We split into groups to do a mock negotiation, and when people came back with their results, no one had done very well, but Sofia had gotten the lowest sales price of all in her negotiation with Noah. As we debriefed the negotiation as a class, I said, "So Sofia, what happened?"

She smiled and shrugged. "So what happened was that I negotiated with Noah and he beat me badly. But I'm not surprised. He's a Jew," she said by way of explanation.

I stopped cold. Everyone did. You could hear a collective intake of breath throughout the room. It took me a moment to recover, and I prodded Sofia a little bit, sure that she'd realized she'd put her foot in her mouth and would walk her way back from the statement. But she just dug herself deeper. She explained to me and the rest of the class how she worked with a lot of Jewish people, and that they're such savvy and capable businesspeople. This was clearly her way of saying she respected her Jewish colleagues, but the room was having a hard time hearing or accepting the explanation.

Sofia was drawing from hurtful stereotypes, but it was clear to me that wasn't what she was about. She was just genuinely impressed by these friends of hers and connected their money-savvy to their Jewishness. It was a biased and rough-around-the-edges approach, not to mention tone-deaf, but it wasn't grounded in hate. But I knew, given the immediate, collective reaction in the room, that the class couldn't necessarily see what I saw in that moment. The air itself felt clouded by emotion and judgment.

A man in the back raised his hand and said in a shaky voice, "I just need to speak. Sofia, this is just so hurtful." The rest of the class, regardless of their race and ethnicity, piled on, taking turns to apologize to the man for Sofia's statements. Sofia, meanwhile, looked stunned. She'd had no idea what she'd unleashed. She tried to explain herself. I encouraged everyone to be calm, to measure their words, and to hear one another. One woman offered that people who were attacking Sofia were hypocritical because everyone nurses stereotypes in private—Sofia had just made hers public. The man who'd been the first to call out Sofia said he knew Sofia meant no harm, but her statement still hurt.

After a while Noah raised his hand. "Can I say something, since this started with me and Sofia?" Noah turned to Sofia. "I forgive you, Sofia," he said. "And it didn't surprise me," he said to the rest of the class, "because I wear a yarmulke, and I know and expect the reaction that I get when I walk in the room sometimes. I don't like it, but I've unfortunately come to anticipate it."

At that, I suggested that we take a break to let the emotion level of the room come down a little bit. I noticed Sofia grab not just her purse but her bookbag—a sign that she wasn't planning to come back. I think Sofia deeply regretted the course of events but also felt victimized by the way everyone had ganged up to denounce her.

As I suspected, Sofia didn't return. I worried we'd go back to where we started, not talking to one another.

Somehow, we got through the course material for the rest of the afternoon. When we were finishing up, I noted that it had been a long day, and a hard day, and in a lot of ways a really important day. I wasn't just pouring sugar over a bad situation—there were positives. We moved from hurt and pain to forgiveness and understanding. We were living through an intense, divisive period in history, but as a classroom we'd come together and talked through it—we hadn't shut down or shut one another out. That's a real impulse, that urge to think, *Oh, they are so different from me that they'll never understand*. When we do that, we grow further apart. Invite, don't indict. I asked them to return to what we'd talked about all morning, before Sofia's comment, which was empathy. I reminded them we had one less person in the room now, and urged the class to reach out to Sofia if they felt moved to.

I heard later that Sofia did return to class the following week (it wasn't one I taught) and was welcomed with open arms.

In retrospect, that day in class, though exhausting, was both meaningful and remarkable. After all, hard things are hard. Our discussion taught the students more about negotiation than a case study ever could. We moved from pain and judgment to healing.

This was by no means the only time someone made a misplaced statement in one of my classes. Sometimes they dissipate the second they're spoken. But we're in a different moment now—Jews feel targeted. Minorities feel targeted. Women feel targeted. Men feel targeted. The word that keeps coming to mind is *raw*. But when someone is raw, we frequently avoid the subject altogether rather than engage. And that, ultimately, is why I was so happy with the way Sofia's class ended up. We were raw—all of us—and we worked through it. We had the courage to stay at the damn table, and to return to it the next week.

Focus on what works

The most fundamental strategy of politics is to focus on what *isn't* working for voters. That's how campaigns persuade them to vote another way. Pick your issue: health care, immigration, crime—every political challenger is going to say it's broken and that they can fix it.

I wonder, though, if the world really is as bad off as politicians would have us believe, or if maybe we're just not talking about the good news. Because again, that's all I see when I go into the classroom. The many stories I've told in this book don't begin to scratch the surface of the transformations I've seen in students over the years. It's not just that they've learned to get better deals (although they do), but they grow, they change, they self-correct, they change the ways they relate to and engage with others. They are kinder to themselves, and they are kinder to others. I've met very few people who are dead-set in their ways. And that is something to be very hopeful about, no matter the nature of the conversation. They are what keep me coming back, and what will always keep me coming back . . . because they prove to me that negotiation works.

acknowledgments

This was a daunting and demanding process from beginning to end, with stories that span so many different chapters of my life. As such, there are far too many people to thank, so here's a collective note of gratitude to my family and friends—my tribe and constant source of inspiration. A special thanks to my sister, who encouraged me to share my story and not worry about judgment. That conversation was everything!

A few people have been particularly instrumental in making this book possible. A big thanks to Howard Yoon for your encouragement and support. This book was an idea for so long, with many different iterations. I appreciate you walking alongside me as we discovered the right direction for the right time. Thanks to everyone on the Avery team who helped shape and advance this book. A special recognition for my editor, Lucia Watson, for her discerning insight, thoughtfulness, and vision. I'm so grateful to my early readers, Jill Hudson and Ken Shropshire, for their smart and gracious feedback. Jenna Free, what can I say? We've learned and grown together. Through it all, you've been patient and open-minded, boosting me and challenging me when I needed it the most.

Teaching was never something I imagined pursuing. Ken Shropshire, I have no idea to this day what you saw or how you knew, but you believed. You encouraged me to teach even when I thought it was improbable. Thank you for friendship and mentorship and opening the doors for me at Wharton.

I am forever grateful to John F. W. Rogers and my entire Goldman Sachs Foundation family for their support and encouragement. Special thanks to Rita McGlone and my colleagues at the Wharton School for inviting me to teach in the Goldman Sachs *10,000 Women* initiative at the American University in Cairo. That program was life-changing in more ways than I can count.

I'm so thankful to the many people who agreed to share their stories in this book, allowing my readers to learn from your triumphs and obstacles. You were generous with your time and unwavering in your honesty.

Last but not least, I want to thank my students, who always commit to their learning with courage and conviction. Their experiences are at the heart of this book. They know me best and see me in my power and, often, my vulnerability. Thank you for opening my heart and mind and enriching my life in so many ways.

notes

Chapter 1: How Our Stories Sell Us Short

22 **Margarita Mayo . . . wrote in the _Harvard Business Review_:** Margarita Mayo, "The Gender Gap in Feedback and Self-Perception," _Harvard Business Review_, August 31, 2016, https://hbr.org/2016/08/the-gender-gap -in-feedback-and-self-perception.

23 **"The data is pretty grim":** Katty Kay and Claire Shipman, _The Confidence Code: The Science and Art of Self-Assurance—What Women Should Know_ (New York: HarperCollins, 2014), xviii.

23 **they see more incidents as worthy of apology:** Rachael Rettner, "Study Reveals Why Women Apologize So Much," _Live Science_, September 27, 2010, https://www.livescience.com/8698-study-reveals-women-apologize.html.

31 **"We are never in a room":** Oprah Winfrey, "Wes Moore: Is Your Job Your Life's Purpose?," podcast audio, _Oprah's SuperSoul Conversations_, OWN, May 21, 2018, https://podcasts.apple.com/gb/podcast/wes-moore-is-your-job -your-lifes-purpose/id1264843400?i=1000411964463.

31 **the more positive our narrative, the better our results:** Daniel J. Tomasulo and James O. Pawelski, "Happily Ever After: The Use of Stories to Promote Positive Interventions," _Psychology_ 3, no. 12A (December 2012): 1191, http://dx.doi.org/10.4236/psych.2012.312A176; Martin Seligman et al., "Positive Psychology Progress: Empirical Validation of Interventions," _American Psychologist_ 60, no. 5 (2005): 410, http://dx.doi.org/10.1037 /0003-066X.60.5.410.

Chapter 2: When We Undercut Ourselves to Please Others

42 **The men's requests for more money exceeded the women's by _nine to one_:** Linda Babcock et al., "Nice Girls Don't Ask," _Harvard Business Review_, October 2003, https://hbr.org/2003/10/nice-girls-dont-ask.

43 **a correlation between sociotropy and eating more around others:** Julie J. Exline et al., "People-Pleasing through Eating: Sociotropy Predicts Greater Eating in Response to Perceived Social Pressure," *Journal of Social and Clinical Psychology* 31, no. 2 (2012): 169, https://doi.org/10.1521 /jscp.2012.31.2.169.

44 **the solution is redefining what it means to be a good manager:** Elizabeth Grace Saunders, "Stop Being a People Pleaser," *Harvard Business Review*, October 30, 2012, https://hbr.org/2012/10/stop-being-a-people-pleaser.

50 **He aimed to get rejected every single day:** Alex Spiegel, "By Making a Game out of Rejection, a Man Conquers Fear," *Morning Edition*, NPR, January 16, 2015, https://www.npr.org/sections/health-shots/2015/01/16 /377239011/by-making-a-game-out-of-rejection-a-man-conquers-fear? t=1556281440846.

Chapter 4: Getting the *How* Wrong

77 **the chief "stays behind the flock":** Joe Campolo, "Mandela—Master Negotiator," Campolo, Middleton & McCormick, LLP blog, March 27, 2014, http://cmmllp.com/mandela-master-negotiator/.

79 **"five-second rule":** David McCandless, "51 Favorite Facts You've Always Believed That Are Actually False," *Reader's Digest*, https://www.rd.com /culture/false-facts-everyone-believes/, accessed May 25, 2019.

80 **negotiating the purchase of Lucasfilm:** PON Staff, "The Star Wars Negotiations and Trust at the Negotiating Table," Harvard Law School, *Program on Negotiation* (PON) blog, May 7, 2019, https://www.pon .harvard.edu/daily/business-negotiations/a-forceful-deal-george-lucas -puts-his-trust-in-disney/.

84 **the achievements of women are viewed more critically:** Madeline E. Heilman et al., "Penalties for Success: Reactions to Women Who Succeed at Male Gender-Typed Tasks," *Journal of Applied Psychology* 89, no. 3 (2004): 416, http://dx.doi.org/10.1037/0021-9010.89.3.416; Madeline E. Heilman and Michelle C. Haynes, "No Credit Where Credit Is Due: Attributional Rationalization of Women's Success in Male-Female Teams," *Journal of Applied Psychology* 90, no. 5 (2005): 905, http://dx.doi.org/10.1037 /0021-9010.90.5.905; Madeline Heilman, "Gender Stereotypes and Workplace Bias," *Research in Organizational Behavior* 32 (2012): 113, https:// doi.org/10.1016/j.riob.2012.11.003; Rhea E. Steinpreis, Katie A. Anders, and Dawn Ritzke, "The Impact of Gender on the Review of the Curricula Vitae of Job Applicants and Tenure Candidates: A National Empirical

Study," *Sex Roles* 41, no. 7–8 (1999): 509–510, https://link.springer.com /article/10.1023/A:1018839203698.

Chapter 5: The Power of an Open Mind

97 **64 percent of people who supported same-sex marriage chose to take less money so as not to have to read the opposing view:** Jeremy Frimer, Linda J. Skitka, and Matt Motyl, "Liberals and Conservatives Are Similarly Motivated to Avoid Exposure to One Another's Opinions," *Journal of Experimental Social Psychology* 72, no. 1–12 (2017): 10, https:// papers.ssrn.com/sol3/papers.cfm?abstract_id=2953780.

105 **"Our brains are better at processing faces that evoke a sense of familiarity":** Jennifer Eberhardt, *Biased: Uncovering the Hidden Prejudice That Shapes What We See, Think, and Do* (New York: Viking, 2019), 14.

105 **bias is triggered by stress:** Eberhardt, *Biased*, 85.

105 **change their foot pursuit policies:** Alisa Chang, "MacArthur Genius Recipient Jennifer Eberhardt Discusses Her New Book 'Biased,'" *All Things Considered*, NPR, March 26, 2019, https://www.npr.org/2019/03/26 /706969408/macarthur-genius-recipient-jennifer-eberhardt-discusses -her-new-book-biased.

107 **that percentage rises to 87 percent:** Erik Larson, "New Research: Diversity + Inclusion = Better Decision Making At Work," *Forbes*, September 21, 2017, https://www.forbes.com/sites/eriklarson/2017/09/21 /new-research-diversity-inclusion-better-decision-making-at -work/#3fca39af4cbf.

107 **"nonhomogenous teams are simply smarter":** David Rock and Heidi Grant, "Why Diverse Teams Are Smarter," *Harvard Business Review*, November 4, 2016, https://hbr.org/2016/11/why-diverse-teams-are -smarter.

108 **how offensive the clothing designs were:** Anne d'Innocenzio, "Gucci, Prada, H&M—Fashion Brands Blunder over Racial Sensitivity," *Stuff*, February 18, 2019, https://www.stuff.co.nz/business/world /110664121/gucci-prada-hm—fashion-brands-blunder-over -racial-sensitivity.

108 **Participants didn't want to hear the opposing position:** Tom Jacobs, "Why We Shut Ourselves Off from Opposing Viewpoints," *Pacific Standard Magazine*, June 14, 2017, https://psmag.com/news/why-we-shut-ourselves -off-from-opposing-viewpoints.

110 ***Fresh Air* host Terry Gross:** Jolie Kerr, "How to Talk to People, According to Terry Gross," *New York Times*, November 17, 2018, https://www.nytimes.com/2018/11/17/style/self-care/terry-gross-conversation-advice.html.

110 **"The difference between appreciation and flattery?":** Dale Carnegie, *How to Win Friends and Influence People*, rev. ed. (New York: Simon & Schuster, 1981), 30.

111 **how much curiosity like this matters in personal relationships:** Patricia Donovan, "Study Finds That Curiosity Is Key to Personal Growth in Many Spheres, Including Intimate Relationships," University at Buffalo, News Center, December 16, 2002, http://www.buffalo.edu/news/releases/2002/12/5996.html.

118 **a dress that some viewers swore was white and gold:** Jonathan Mahler, "The White and Gold (No, Blue and Black!) Dress That Melted the Internet," *New York Times*, February 27, 2015, https://www.nytimes.com/2015/02/28/business/a-simple-question-about-a-dress-and-the-world-weighs-in.html.

Chapter 6: The Power of Empathy

120 **"Let's talk, Eddie":** L. Gregory Jones, "Leadership as Loving Enemies," *Faith and Leadership*, January 4, 2009, https://www.faithandleadership.com/content/leadership-loving-enemies.

120 **Lt. Jack Cambria prizes empathy as a critical negotiation tool:** Pervaiz Shallwani, "Life Lessons from the NYPD's Top Hostage Negotiator," *Wall Street Journal*, August 28, 2015, https://www.wsj.com/articles/life-lessons-from-the-nypds-top-hostage-negotiator-1440726792.

121 **influence "is all about relationship building":** Gary Noesner, "The Best Books on Negotiating and the FBI Recommended by Gary Noesner," *Five Books*, https://fivebooks.com/best-books/gary-noesner-on-negotiating-and-the-fbi/, accessed May 26, 2019.

121 **"I believe that's what Israeli parents would want for these kids":** Ben Rhodes, *The World As It Is* (New York: Random House, 2018), 201.

132 **a group of researchers studied reactions to opening offers:** PON Staff, "Win Win Negotiation—Managing Your Counterpart's Satisfaction," Harvard Law School, *Program on Negotiation* (PON) blog, December 24, 2018, https://www.pon.harvard.edu/daily/win-win-daily/win-win-negotiations-managing-your-counterparts-satisfaction/.

133 **"a negotiation isn't about only money":** Michael S. Hopkins, "How to

Negotiate Practically Everything," February 1, 1989, https://www.inc
.com/magazine/19890201/5526.html.

135 **"both sides were making a sacrifice"**: Charalambos Vlachoutsicos,
"Empathetic Negotiation Saved My Company," *Harvard Business Review*,
October 24, 2013, https://hbr.org/2013/10/empathetic-negotiation
-saved-my-company.

Chapter 7: Wherever You Are, Be There Fully

139 **she noticed everything about her counterpart, Iranian foreign minister
Javad Zarif:** Wendy Sherman, *Not for the Faint of Heart* (New York:
PublicAffairs, 2018), 43.

139 **more distractible than goldfish:** Kevin McSpadden, "You Now Have a
Shorter Attention Span Than a Goldfish," *Time*, May 14, 2015, http://time
.com/3858309/attention-spans-goldfish/.

144 **the mere presence of your phone is distracting:** Adrian F. Ward et al.,
"Brain Drain: The Mere Presence of One's Own Smartphone Reduces
Available Cognitive Capacity," *Journal of the Association for Consumer Research*
2, no. 2 (2017), https://www.journals.uchicago.edu/doi/full/10.1086/691462.

144 **they checked their phones an average of every twelve minutes *while on
vacation*:** "Americans Don't Want to Unplug from Phones While on
Vacation, Despite Latest Digital Detox Trend," press release, Asurion.com,
May 17, 2018, https://www.asurion.com/about/press-releases/americans
-dont-want-to-unplug-from-phones-while-on-vacation-despite-latest
-digital-detox-trend/.

145 **"you remember who you were as a reader":** Maryanne Wolf, *Reader Come
Home: The Reading Brain in a Digital World* (New York: HarperCollins, 2018), 2.

150 **"I saw my expression as a stranger might perceive it":** Michelle Obama,
Becoming (New York: Crown, 2018), 61.

150 **"It was okay, in other words, to be myself":** Obama, *Becoming*, 89.

155 **the party who was angry did not in fact claim any more value for
themselves:** Keith Allred et al., "The Influence of Anger and Compassion
on Negotiation Performance," *Organizational Behavior and Human Decision
Processes* 70, no. 3 (1997), https://doi.org/10.1006/obhd.1997.2705.

155 **more likely to walk away:** Jeremy A. Yip and Martin Schweinsberg,
"Infuriating Impasses: Angry Expressions Increase Exiting Behavior in
Negotiations," *Social Psychological and Personality Science* 8, no. 6 (2017),
https://doi.org/10.1177/1948550616683021.

Chapter 8: Assume Abundance

164 **"almost universally reviled"**: Olga Khazan, "Why Do Women Bully Each Other at Work?" *The Atlantic*, September 2017, https://www.theatlantic.com /magazine/archive/2017/09/the-queen-bee-in-the-corner-office/534213/. Allison S. Gabriel et al., "Further Understanding Incivility in the Workplace: The Effects of Gender, Agency, and Communion," *Journal of Applied Psychology* 103, no. 4 (April 2018): 362–382, http://psycnet.apa.org /doiLanding?doi=10.1037%2Fapl0000289.

169 **"to bring people to their senses rather than to their knees"**: Neil Katz and Kevin McNulty, "Interest-Based Negotiation," Maxwell School of Citizenship and Public Policy, 1995, https://www.maxwell.syr.edu /uploadedFiles/parcc/cmc/Interested-Based%20Negotiation%20NK.pdf.

176 **"ethical fading"**: PON Staff, "Why Is Sincerity Important? How to Avoid Deception in Negotiation," Harvard Law School, *Program on Negotiation* (PON) blog, January 7, 2019, https://www.pon.harvard.edu/daily /conflict-resolution/why-we-succumb-to-deception-in-negotiation/.

176 **Because of Morgan's integrity, Carnegie was loyal to him**: Michael Benoliel, *Done Deal* (Avon, MA: Platinum Press, 2005), 114.

180 **"to develop a nice relationship with the public"**: Paul B. Brown and Michael S. Hopkins, "How to Negotiate Practically Anything," interview with Bob Woolf, *Inc.*, February 1, 1989, https://www.inc.com/magazine /19890201/5526.html.

182 **"She literally convinced the union"**: Fast Company Staff, "Fresh Copy: How Ursula Burns Reinvented Xerox," *Fast Company*, November 19, 2011, https://www.fastcompany.com/1793533/fresh-copy-how-ursula -burns-reinvented-xerox.

183 **people share more when others reveal sensitive information**: Leslie K. John, "How to Negotiate with a Liar," *Harvard Business Review*, July–August 2016, https://hbr.org/2016/07/how-to-negotiate-with-a-liar.

183 **the listener doesn't even notice that they've deflected the question**: John, "How to Negotiate with a Liar."

Chapter 9: Claiming Your Power

194 **Most of the decision makers on Wall Street**: Sallie Krawcheck, *Own It: The Power of Women at Work* (New York: Crown Business, 2017), 7.

- 240 -

195 **"We had shaken those clients' confidence in us"**: Krawcheck, *Own It*, 4.

196 **"you take the gender and the race differences and use them as a strength"**: Ursula Burns, "Ursula Burns: First Woman to Run a Fortune 500 Company," *Time*, http://time.com/collection/firsts/4883099/ursula -burns-firsts/, accessed May 28, 2019.

196 **Kyle MacDonald, who traded a paper clip all the way up to a house:** "From Paper-Clip to House in 14 Trades," *CBC News*, July 7, 2006, https:// www.cbc.ca/news/canada/from-paper-clip-to-house-in-14-trades -1.573973.

204 **a turning point came when frustrated tears ran down her face:** Sherman, *Not for the Faint of Heart*, xvi.

210 **"identify a similarity you share in common, then begin negotiating"**: Robert Cialdini, "Principles of Persuasion," video, *Influence at Work*, https://www.influenceatwork.com/principles-of-persuasion/, accessed June 1, 2019.

211 **"not an obstacle but a point of commonality"**: Sherman, *Not for the Faint of Heart*, 39.

212 **force yourself to smile:** Nicole Spector, "Smiling Can Trick Your Brain into Happiness—and Boost Your Health," *NBC News*, November 28, 2017, https://www.nbcnews.com/better/health/smiling-can-trick-your-brain -happiness-boost-your-health-ncna822591.

212 **if your counterpart believes you're acting as a way to gain status:** Michael Schaerer, Martin Schweinsberg, and Roderick Swaab, "Imaginary Alternatives: The Effects of Mental Simulation on Powerless Negotiators," *Journal of Personality and Social Psychology* 115, no. 1 (2018), https://psycnet .apa.org/record/2018-13326-001.

212 **when you stand in a dominant posture:** Amy Cuddy, "Your Body Language May Shape Who You Are," TED Talk video, 2012, https://www .ted.com/talks/amy_cuddy_your_body_language_shapes_who_you_are ?language=en.

213 **"to convince others we need to convince ourselves"**: Amy Cuddy, *Presence: Bringing Your Boldest Self to Your Biggest Challenges* (New York: Little, Brown, 2015), 41.

213 **simply imagine that you have more power:** Schaerer et al., "Imaginary Alternatives."

Chapter 10: How Negotiation Can Save Democracy

218 **the number of people who feel lonely**: Laura Entis, "Loneliness Is a Modern Day Epidemic," *Fortune*, June 22, 2016, http://fortune.com/2016 /06/22/loneliness-is-a-modern-day-epidemic/.

219 **"difficult conversations among family members who initially disagreed"**: Karin Tamerius, "How to Have a Conversation with Your Angry Uncle over the Holidays," *New York Times*, November 18, 2019, https://www.nytimes.com/interactive/2018/11/18/opinion/thanksgiving -family-argue-chat-bot.html.

221 **the canvasser asked him at the end of the conversation if he supported gay marriage**: Ira Glass, "The Incredible Rarity of Changing Your Mind," podcast audio, *This American Life*, WBEZ Chicago, April 24, 2015, https:// www.thisamericanlife.org/555/the-incredible-rarity-of-changing-your -mind. (Note that although a study used in this episode was later discredited, the canvasser's conversation with the voter remains accurate.)

222 **"I am a white male," he said, "and I am prejudiced"**: Heather McGhee, "'What Can I Do to Change? You Know? To Be a Better American?'" Interview with Heather McGhee, CSPAN's *Washington Journal* via YouTube, August 20, 2016, https://www.youtube.com/watch?v=BsUa7eCgE_U; Daniel Smith, "A Friendship for a More Tolerant America," *New Yorker*, December 25, 2016, https://www.newyorker.com/magazine/2017/01/02 /a-friendship-for-a-more-tolerant-america.

223 **Galileo then discovered four moons orbiting Jupiter**: Todd Rose and Ogi Ogas, *Dark Horse: Achieving Success through the Pursuit of Fulfillment* (New York: HarperOne, 2018).

224 **"no colored bathrooms in this building"**: *Hidden Figures*, 20th Century Fox, released December 25, 2016.

225 **"asking our partners to assume experiences they have likely never had"**: Kimberly Harrington, "When Will It Be Times Up for Motherhood and Marriage?," *Medium*, July 20, 2018, https://medium.com/s/story/when -will-it-be-times-up-for-motherhood-and-marriage-2766d311bfae.

227 **those who read literary fiction were more empathetic**: David Comer Kidd and Emanuele Castano, "Reading Literary Fiction Improves Theory of Mind," *Science* 342, no. 6156, DOI: 10.1126/science.1239918.

227 **"one can much more easily talk about a movie"**: John Guida, "How Movies Can Change Our Minds," *New York Times*, February 4, 2015, https://op-talk .blogs.nytimes.com/2015/02/04/how-movies-can-change-our-minds/.

index